delicious.

ove to Cook

SIMPLY DELICIOUS RECIPES TO SHARE

delicious.
Love to Cook

140 SIMPLY DELICIOUS RECIPES TO SHARE

Valli Little

WELCOME

It's true – I really *do* love to cook. I never get tired of it,
despite having done it professionally and for pleasure for more
than 40 years. I'm continually inspired by new produce and ideas, and
love putting my own spin on things. When people ask me the reason for
ABC *delicious.* magazine's ongoing success, I tell them that first and foremost
we love to inspire, but we also like to make things easy for the cook. Not that
our recipes are basic; quite the contrary. For us, it's all about having fun in the
kitchen, creating dishes that look and taste amazing without too much stress.
There are more than 140 recipes in this book, including some great essentials
that I like to have in my pantry, such as an onion marmalade that I've used in my 'cheat's'
pissaladiere, which is also great added to quiches or as a condiment for sausages and
steaks. There's a lemon curd that's perfect as a quick cake or tart filling, which also works
a treat in my lemon tiramisu (although it's so good, it may not last that long in the fridge).
There's even a lesson on boiling an egg. It's surprising how many people get it wrong;
but once you know the basics, the whole wonderful world of cooking opens up for you.
You'll find plenty of ideas for quick midweek dinners, from Greek lamb with
orzo to the world's easiest tomato pasta sauce, as well as impressive dishes for
entertaining – think Massaman roast chicken or chocolate silk tart with chocolate
glacé oranges. Whichever you choose, they're all dishes that we hope
you'll *Love to Cook*, and your family and friends will love to share
– which is really what good food is all about.

Valli

CONTENTS

Quail eggs

Milk

Yoghurt

EGGS & DAIRY

FLASH-FRIED RICE WITH FRIED EGG AND TOGARASHI

2 tbs vegetable oil
2 garlic cloves,
    finely chopped
1 long red chilli, seeds
    removed, finely chopped
2 tsp grated ginger
100g mangetout,
    trimmed and sliced
700g cooked white rice
1 tsp caster sugar
2 tsp fish sauce
2 tbs light soy sauce
50g roasted unsalted
    peanuts, finely chopped
4 spring onions, thinly
    sliced on an angle, plus
    extra shredded, to serve
4 eggs
1 tbs shichimi togarashi
Coriander sprigs, to serve

Heat a wok or large frypan over medium-high heat. Add 1 tbs oil and stir-fry garlic, chilli and ginger for 15 seconds or until fragrant. Add mangetout and stir-fry for 1 minute, then add rice and stir-fry for 1 minute or until heated through. Add sugar, fish and soy sauces, peanuts and spring onion, stirring until sugar dissolves. Remove pan from heat, cover and set aside.

Heat remaining 1 tbs oil in a separate frypan over medium-high heat. Break eggs into pan and fry until cooked to your liking.

Divide rice among 4 bowls, top with a fried egg and serve each sprinkled with 1 tsp shichimi togarashi, coriander and shredded spring onion. **Serves 4**

HERBED SCRAMBLED EGG, PROSCIUTTO & CHEVRE CROSTINI

12 slices ciabatta

2 tbs extra virgin olive oil, plus extra, to brush

4 eggs

60ml single cream

40g unsalted butter

1 heaped tsp of finely chopped mixed herbs (such as flat-leaf parsley and chives), plus extra to serve

Soft goat's cheese (chevre) prosciutto, chopped tomatoes and rocket leaves, to serve

Heat a chargrill pan to high. Brush bread on both sides with a little olive oil, then cook, turning once, until both sides are well charred. Set aside and keep warm.

Lightly whisk eggs and cream together in a bowl. Season with sea salt and freshly ground black pepper.

Heat 1 tbs oil and 20g butter in a saucepan over medium heat. Add eggs, then reduce heat to low and cook, stirring gently, for 3-4 minutes until soft curds form. Remove pan from heat, then stir through herbs and remaining 20g butter.

Serve eggs with chargrilled ciabatta, goat's cheese, prosciutto, tomato and rocket, drizzle with remaining 1 tbs olive oil and sprinkle with extra herbs. **Serves 4**

BAKED RICOTTA WITH ROASTED TOMATO, PEAS & TRUFFLE OIL

250g cherry tomatoes, halved
Olive oil, to drizzle
3 tsp chopped thyme leaves
500g fresh ricotta, drained
1 tsp chilli flakes
80g grated parmesan
150g fresh or frozen peas
25g wild rocket leaves
2 tsp truffle oil, plus extra to drizzle

Preheat the oven to 120°C (gas mark 1/2)

Place tomatoes on a baking tray and drizzle with a little olive oil. Season with sea salt and freshly ground black pepper and sprinkle with 1 tsp thyme. Roast for 1 1/2 hours or until tomatoes start to collapse. Remove and set aside.

Increase oven to 180°C (gas mark 4). Grease 4 x 200ml ramekins.

Place ricotta, chilli, three-quarters of the parmesan and remaining 2 tsp thyme in a bowl, season and stir to combine. Divide ricotta mixture among prepared dishes, pressing down gently, then place on a baking tray. Bake for 15 minutes or until slightly puffed and golden.

Meanwhile, cook fresh peas for 5 minutes or frozen for 2 minutes in a pan of boiling salted water. Drain and toss warm peas with truffle oil and remaining 20g parmesan, then lightly mash with a fork.

To serve, invert the baked ricottas onto individual plates, then top with peas, roasted tomatoes and rocket, and drizzle with extra truffle oil. **Serves 4**

CHINESE OMELETTES WITH BARBECUE DUCK

8 eggs
2 garlic cloves,
 finely chopped
2 tsp grated ginger
2 tsp rice wine (Shaohsing)
300g cooked, sliced
 Chinese barbecue duck
100g mangetout, trimmed,
 finely sliced on an angle
6 spring onions,
 finely shredded
100g beansprouts, trimmed
1 long red chilli, seeds
 removed, finely shredded
1/2 bunch each coriander
 and mint, leaves picked
Juice of 1 lime
80ml vegetable oil
Oyster sauce, to drizzle

Lightly whisk eggs in a bowl with the garlic, ginger and rice wine.

In a large bowl, combine duck, mangetout, onion, beansprouts, chilli, and coriander and mint leaves. Add lime juice to taste, season with sea salt and freshly ground black pepper. Set aside.

Heat 2 tbs oil in a 20cm non-stick frypan over medium-high heat. Add half the egg mixture, tipping the pan gently and pulling the omelette away from the sides of the pan until it has just set. Transfer to a plate and keep warm, then repeat with remaining oil and egg mixture. Top each omelette with the duck and salad mixture, drizzle with a little oyster sauce and roll up to serve.

Serves 4 as a main course; or serve as part of a Chinese banquet

FRIED EGGS WITH BACON JAM

500g smoked bacon, rind
    removed, finely chopped
1 onion, finely chopped
4 garlic cloves,
    finely chopped
125g dark brown sugar
60ml bourbon
125ml freshly brewed
    espresso
2 tbs sherry or balsamic
    vinegar
60ml maple syrup
4 eggs

Bacon jam is the latest craze out of the USA and, while the combination of ingredients sounds bizarre, it's delicious, and a jar in the fridge won't last long. If you prefer a finer texture to your jam, pulse it a few times using a food processor before transferring to a jar. Jam will keep, stored in the fridge, for up to 1 week.

Cook bacon in a frypan over medium heat, stirring occasionally, for 3-4 minutes until most of the fat has rendered. Remove bacon with a slotted spoon and drain on paper towel. Pour off the melted fat and reserve, leaving 1 tbs fat in the pan.

Reduce heat to medium-low, then add the onion and cook, stirring occasionally, for 5-6 minutes until golden. Add garlic and stir to combine, then add sugar, bourbon, espresso, vinegar, maple syrup, cooked bacon and 125ml water.

Season with sea salt and freshly ground black pepper, then increase heat to medium-high and bring to a simmer. Reduce heat to low and cook, stirring occasionally, for 1 hour or until the mixture is a jammy consistency. Makes about 700g.

Heat a little of the reserved bacon fat in a frypan and fry eggs to your liking. Serve with spoonfuls of bacon jam. **Serves 4**

PROPER CUSTARD

Whisk 4 egg yolks, 60g caster sugar and 2 tsp cornflour in a heatproof bowl.

Combine 600ml milk, 100ml single cream and a scraped vanilla pod and seeds in a saucepan. Bring almost to the boil over medium heat.

Slowly pour hot milk mixture into egg yolk mixture, gently whisking to combine.

Return custard to pan and stir over a very low heat with a wooden spoon for 3-4 minutes until slightly thickened and smooth.

To make creme patissiere, use 2 tbs cornflour and cook for an extra 1 minute. It will thicken further when chilled.

PERFECT BOILED EGGS

Place room-temperature eggs in a small saucepan, cover with cold water and bring to the boil over high heat.

Immediately reduce heat to low and simmer for 3 minutes for soft-boiled, 4 minutes for a set white and creamy yolk, and 5 minutes for a set white and yolk (hard-boiled).

MALAYSIAN-STYLE PRAWN & EGG LAKSA

1 bunch coriander, leaves
  picked, stalks and
  roots reserved
1 tbs vegetable oil
4 shallots, thinly sliced
1 lemongrass stalk (inner
  core only), finely chopped
1 long red chilli, seeds
  removed, thinly sliced
8 kaffir limes leaves,
  finely shredded
200g good-quality
  laksa paste
1L fish or chicken stock
270ml can coconut milk
2 tbs fish sauce
2 tbs grated palm sugar
  or brown sugar
250g vermicelli rice noodles
800g raw prawns, peeled
  (tails intact), deveined
2 tbs lime juice
4 soft-boiled eggs, halved
100g beansprouts, trimmed
15g fried Asian shallots

Finely chop the coriander stalks and roots. Heat oil in a wok over medium-high heat. Add shallots, lemongrass, chilli, chopped coriander stalks and roots and half the kaffir lime leaves. Stir-fry for 1 minute or until fragrant. Add laksa paste and stir-fry for a few seconds until fragrant and combined. Add stock, coconut milk, fish sauce and sugar, and bring to the boil, then reduce heat to medium-low and simmer for 10 minutes.

Meanwhile, soak noodles in boiling water according to the packet instructions, then drain.

Add prawns to laksa broth and cook for a further 2-3 minutes until cooked through. Stir through lime juice.

Divide noodles among 4 bowls, then pour over laksa. Top each bowl with two halves of hard-boiled egg, beansprouts, fried Asian shallots, coriander leaves and remaining kaffir lime. **Serves 4**

EGG & MEATBALL SHAKSHOUKA

60ml olive oil

1 onion, finely chopped

2 garlic cloves,
 finely chopped

2 tbs good-quality
 red harissa paste

1 cinnamon quill

2 x 400g cans chopped
 tomatoes

310ml beef stock

500g lamb mince

2 tbs chopped coriander,
 plus extra sprigs to serve

100g fresh breadcrumbs

4 eggs

Grilled Turkish bread,
 to serve

While this Middle Eastern dish is usually served as a breakfast of eggs in a spicy tomato base, I've added little lamb meatballs to make it more substantial. Make sure you leave the egg yolks runny and serve plenty of grilled Turkish bread to dip and swirl through the sauce. Shakshouka means 'all mixed up', after all!

Heat 1 tbs oil in a frypan over medium heat. Add half the onion and cook for 1-2 minutes, then add half the garlic and 1 tbs harissa paste and cook for a further 1-2 minutes until fragrant. Add cinnamon, tomato and stock, stir to combine and season with sea salt and freshly ground black pepper. Reduce heat to medium-low and simmer for 30 minutes.

Meanwhile, combine mince, coriander, breadcrumbs and remaining onion, garlic and 1 tbs harissa in a bowl. Season, then form tablespoonfuls of lamb mixture into walnut-sized balls. Refrigerate until ready to cook.

Preheat the oven to 200°C (gas mark 6). Heat 1 tbs oil over medium heat and cook half the meatballs for 3-4 minutes, turning, until golden all over and almost cooked. Drain on paper towel. Repeat with remaining 1 tbs oil and meatballs.

Divide meatballs among 4 x 500ml ovenproof dishes or place in a 1.5L-capacity baking dish, then pour over the hot tomato sauce. Form a well in the centre of each dish and crack an egg into it. If using a large dish, make 4 wells in the tomato mixture. Bake for 8-10 minutes until the egg whites are just cooked but the yolks are still runny.

Serve with sliced grilled Turkish bread. **Serves 4**

BUTTERMILK PUDDINGS

1 vanilla bean, split,
  seeds scraped
75g caster sugar
600ml double cream
4 gold gelatine leaves
500ml buttermilk

Lightly oil 4 x 250ml moulds.

Place vanilla pod and seeds, sugar and 400ml cream in a saucepan over medium heat, stirring gently until sugar dissolves.

Meanwhile, soak gelatine in cold water for 5 minutes to soften. Squeeze excess water from gelatine, then add to the hot cream, stirring to dissolve. Strain mixture into a bowl set over a bowl of ice to allow the mixture to chill slightly. Lightly whisk remaining 200ml cream to soft peaks, then gently fold into the mixture with the buttermilk. Pour into prepared moulds, then refrigerate for 4-6 hours until set.

To serve, invert puddings onto plates. **Serves 4**

RICE PUDDING WITH STRAWBERRY SYRUP

1L full-cream milk
200g arborio rice
110g caster sugar
1 cinnamon quill
1 vanilla bean, split,
  seeds scraped
60ml double cream

Strawberry syrup
400g strawberries,
  hulled, halved if large
330g caster sugar
Juice of 1 lemon
1 vanilla bean, split,
  seeds scraped
2 tsp arrowroot
  or cornflour

Place milk, rice, sugar, cinnamon and vanilla pod and seeds in a saucepan over medium heat. Bring to a simmer, then reduce heat to low and cook, stirring occasionally, for 20-25 minutes until rice is almost cooked. Remove from heat, cover and set aside for 15 minutes. Stir in cream.

Meanwhile, to make strawberry syrup, place all the ingredients, except for the arrowroot, in a saucepan over low heat and cook, stirring occasionally, for 5-6 minutes. Combine arrowroot with 2 tsp cold water, then add to strawberry mixture and cook for a further 2 minutes or until slightly thickened. Cool. Syrup will keep in an airtight container in the fridge for up to 2 weeks.

Serve strawberry syrup with the rice pudding. **Serves 4**

THREE MILKS CAKE

3 eggs, separated
1 tbs vanilla extract
200g golden caster sugar
150g self-raising flour, sifted
1 tsp baking powder
125ml evaporated milk
125ml condensed milk
125ml full-cream milk
200ml double cream,
   whisked to soft peaks
Seasonal berries, to serve

This is my version of the classic Latin American *tres leches* (literally, 'three milks'). The sponge base soaks up the combined milks to form an extremely rich, luscious sweet, traditionally slathered with a thick layer of whipped cream. In Mexico, maraschino cherries are a favoured topping, but I've used fresh, tart berries to balance the richness.

Preheat the oven to 150°C (gas mark 2). Grease and line base and side of a 20cm springform cake pan.

Using an electric mixer, whisk egg whites on low speed for 1 minute or until frothy. Add egg yolks and beat on medium speed for 1 minute. Add vanilla and sugar, and beat for 1 minute. Add flour and baking powder, and beat for a further 1 minute or until just combined. Transfer batter to cake pan, gently smoothing surface, then bake for 35-40 minutes until golden. Cool cake in pan for 15-20 minutes, then turn out onto a serving plate with a rim.

Meanwhile, combine the three milks in a jug, then slowly pour milk mixture over the cake, allowing it to soak in.

Serve slices of cake topped with a dollop of whipped cream and seasonal berries. **Serves 6**

SOUPS & STARTERS

First impressions are lasting impressions.

Soup of
the day

SPICED CARROT SOUP WITH COCONUT CREAM

1 tbs olive oil

1 onion, finely chopped

2 garlic cloves,
   finely chopped

1 small red chilli, seeds
   removed, chopped

1 tsp grated ginger

500g carrots, chopped

400g sweet potato,
   chopped

4 kaffir lime leaves, 2 whole,
   2 finely shredded

1L chicken stock

2 tbs palm sugar
   or brown sugar

2 tbs fish sauce

Juice of 1/2 lime

200ml coconut cream

150ml double cream

25g toasted shredded
   coconut

Heat oil in a large saucepan over medium heat, add onion and cook for 2 minutes or until softened. Add garlic, chilli, ginger, carrot, sweet potato, whole kaffir lime leaves and stock. Increase heat to high and bring to the boil, then reduce heat to medium-low and simmer for 20-25 minutes until vegetables are tender.

Remove kaffir lime leaves and discard. Set aside mixture in saucepan to cool slightly. Using a blender or stick blender, blend soup to a smooth puree, then return to the pan over medium-low heat. Add palm sugar, fish sauce, lime juice and half the coconut cream, then stir to combine.

Meanwhile, using electric beaters or a balloon whisk, whisk together the double cream and remaining 100ml coconut cream to soft peaks.

To serve, ladle soup into bowls, then swirl through a spoonful of the coconut cream mixture. Top with shredded kaffir lime and toasted shredded coconut. **Serves 4-6**

PORK RILLETTES

1kg piece boneless
  pork belly
3 garlic cloves, bruised
2 bay leaves
2 sprigs thyme
1/2 tsp quatre epices
250ml white wine
2 tbs brandy
Toasted sliced baguette,
  cornichons and preserved
  fruit, to serve

You will need 3 x sterilised 125ml preserving jars. Begin this recipe at least 2 days ahead.

Preheat the oven to 150°C (gas mark 2).

Cut the pork into 4 pieces and place, skin-side up, in a roasting pan just large enough to fit the meat snugly. Sprinkle the skin with salt, then add garlic, herbs and quatre epices to the pan. Add wine, brandy and 250ml water, cover with foil, then cook for 3 1/2 hours until meat is very tender.

Remove pork from oven and set aside to cool slightly. When cool enough to handle, remove skin and discard. Using two forks, shred the meat, then pack into sterilised jars.

Strain pan juices into a jug, then pour over the meat to cover. Seal jars and refrigerate for at least 2 days to allow the flavours to develop. Serve with toasted sliced baguette, cornichons and preserved fruit. **Makes 3 jars**

LAURA ASHLEY SOUP

2 tbs olive oil

1 onion, chopped

1 leek (white part only), chopped

2 celery stalks, chopped

6 beetroot, peeled, chopped

1 carrot, chopped

2 tbs balsamic vinegar

1.5L vegetable stock

$\frac{1}{2}$ tsp cinnamon

$\frac{1}{2}$ tsp nutmeg

200ml creme fraiche or sour cream

2 hard-boiled eggs, peeled, chopped

1 cucumber, peeled, seeds removed, chopped

2 tbs finely chopped dill

Toasted rye croutons, to serve

I've been making this soup for years. The name came about because there was a time when almost everything I bought from the Laura Ashley shop was the most beautiful shade of purple. When the sour cream is swirled through this soup, it turns that very colour and reminds me of those lovely paisley patterns the British designer was so well known for.

Heat oil in a large saucepan over medium-low heat. Add onion, leek and celery, and cook, stirring occasionally, for 2-3 minutes until softened. Add beetroot and carrot, and stir to combine. Add vinegar, stock and spices, then season with sea salt and freshly ground black pepper. Increase heat to medium-high and bring to the boil. Partially cover, then reduce heat to medium and simmer for 1 hour or until the beetroot is tender.

Set aside in saucepan to cool slightly. Using a blender or stick blender, process to a smooth puree. Return soup to the pan over low heat and gently heat through.

Serve with a spoonful of creme fraiche swirled through, with chopped hard-boiled egg, cucumber, dill and croutons scattered over. **Serves 6-8**

TUNA CEVICHE
WITH FRIED TORTILLAS

80ml olive oil

4 mini flour tortillas,
  cut into wedges

300g sashimi-grade tuna

Juice of 2 limes

5 radishes, finely chopped

1 bunch coriander, leaves
  picked, chopped

1/2 pineapple, peeled,
  cored, finely chopped

1 avocado, finely chopped

Seeds of 1 pomegranate

1 shallot, finely chopped

2 cucumbers, peeled, seeds
  removed, finely chopped

1 jalapeno, seeds removed,
  finely chopped

2 tbs pomegranate
  molasses

Heat 60ml oil in a frypan over medium-high heat and shallow-fry tortillas, in batches, until crisp and golden on both sides. Drain on paper towel and set aside until ready to serve.

Finely chop tuna, then place in a non-reactive glass or ceramic bowl. Add lime juice and 1 tsp sea salt, combine gently, then set aside for 30 minutes.

Combine radish, coriander, pineapple, avocado, pomegranate seeds, shallot, cucumber and chilli in a bowl. Drain tuna and add to the bowl with the remaining 1 tbs olive oil and gently toss to combine. Transfer ceviche to small jars or bowls, drizzle with pomegranate molasses and serve with fried tortillas. **Serves 4-6**

PEA PANCAKES WITH CRISP PANCETTA AND SWEET CHILLI SAUCE

160g fresh, podded or
   120g frozen peas
3 eggs
240g fresh ricotta, drained
35g plain flour
1 tbs olive oil, plus
   extra to fry
4 spring onions,
   finely chopped
8 slices round pancetta
   or streaky bacon
Sweet chilli sauce (see
   Essentials, p 45), sour
   cream and pea tendrils
   or watercress sprigs,
   to serve

Cook fresh peas in a saucepan of boiling salted water for
5 minutes or frozen peas for 2 minutes. Drain, refresh in iced
water, then drain well.

Place eggs, ricotta, flour and oil in a food processor. Season
with sea salt and freshly ground black pepper, then process
until smooth. Transfer to a bowl and stir in peas and spring onion
(add a little cold water if the batter is too thick; it should be the
consistency of pancake batter). Set aside for 30 minutes.

Meanwhile, preheat the grill to high.

Place pancetta on a baking tray and grill until crisp and golden.
Drain on paper towel and keep warm.

Heat a little oil in a non-stick frypan over medium-high heat.
Add generous tablespoon of batter to the frypan, in batches,
and cook for 1-2 minutes until golden underneath, then flip
and cook for a further 1-2 minutes. Keep warm and repeat
with remaining batter.

Layer pancakes and pancetta on a serving plate and serve
with sweet chilli sauce, sour cream and pea tendrils. **Serves 4**

PIZZA DOUGH

Combine 7g dried yeast, 1 tsp sugar and 180ml warm water in a bowl and lightly whisk with a fork. Set aside for 10 minutes until frothy.

Meanwhile, sift 300g '00' flour (super-fine Italian pasta flour) or strong plain flour into a large bowl with 1 tsp sea salt and make a well in the centre.

Using a wooden spoon, stir in the yeast mixture and 2 tbs olive oil until the dough just comes together.

Turn out onto a lightly floured surface and knead for 5 minutes or until smooth and elastic (or use a mixer with a dough hook).

Transfer to a clean bowl, cover with a clean tea towel and set aside in a warm place for 1 hour or until doubled in size.

Knock down dough with your fist, then divide into 4 portions. Roll out on a lightly floured surface and transfer to an oiled pizza tray or stone. **Makes 4 x 26cm pizzas**

SWEET CHILLI SAUCE

Place 10 chopped long red chillies, 500ml rice vinegar, 330g caster sugar, 4 chopped garlic cloves and 1 tbs sea salt in a blender and blend to a paste.

Transfer to a saucepan over high heat and bring to the boil, then cook for 5 minutes.

Reduce heat to low and simmer for 20–25 minutes until thickened.

Store in a sterilised jar or airtight container in the fridge for up to 1 month.

TARTIFLETTE PIZZA

450g pink fir apple
  potatoes, peeled
1 garlic clove,
  finely chopped
2 tbs olive oil
8 slices pancetta
  or streaky bacon
1/2 quantity of pizza dough
  (see Essentials, p 44)
  to make 2 x 26cm
  pizza bases
150g Taleggio, torn
1/2 small red onion, sliced
1 tbs finely chopped thyme
1 tbs finely chopped
  flat-leaf parsley

Tartiflette is a French potato and cheese bake, similar to a gratin. Here, I've substituted Taleggio and pancetta for the more traditional Reblochon cheese and lardons, in keeping with the Italian theme.

Preheat the oven to 220°C (gas mark 7). Grease 2 baking trays.

Place potatoes in a saucepan of cold salted water. Bring to the boil and simmer for 5 minutes or until par-boiled. Drain and cool slightly, then cut into 1cm-thick rounds.

Meanwhile, combine garlic and olive oil in a small bowl.

Cook pancetta in a frypan over low heat, turning occasionally, for 10 minutes or until the fat starts to render. Remove pancetta, leaving fat in pan, and drain on paper towel.

Return frypan to the heat and cook potatoes for 1-2 minutes each side until crisp and golden.

Brush pizza bases with garlic oil and place on baking trays. Divide potatoes between the 2 pizza bases, then scatter over Taleggio and onion. Crumble over pancetta, then sprinkle with thyme. Cook for 8-10 minutes until pizza bases are crisp and cheese is melted and bubbling. Serve immediately, scattered with parsley. **Serves 4**

SALMON & AVOCADO VERRINES

2 avocados,
   roughly mashed
2 tbs lemon juice
3 spring onions,
   finely chopped
1$\frac{1}{2}$ cucumbers, peeled,
   seeds removed, finely
   chopped
2 tsp wasabi paste
500g sashimi-grade salmon,
   finely chopped
2 tbs chopped dill, plus
   extra sprigs to serve
150g creme fraiche
   or sour cream
Salmon roe, to serve

The term verrines comes from *verre*, the French word for 'glass'. This style of serving layered ingredients, both sweet and savoury, is *très à la mode* right now.

Place avocado, lemon juice, spring onion, cucumber and 1 tsp wasabi paste in a bowl and stir gently to combine. Season with sea salt and freshly ground black pepper.

In a separate bowl, combine salmon and dill, then season.

Combine creme fraiche with the remaining 1 tsp wasabi paste.

Divide avocado mixture among 6 x 200ml glasses, then top with salmon mixture. To serve, add a spoonful of creme fraiche mixture, a little salmon roe and extra dill sprigs. **Serves 6**

LAMB & HALOUMI SAUSAGE ROLLS

500g lamb mince
70g fresh breadcrumbs
90g mint jelly
1 tbs finely chopped mint
200g haloumi, grated
2 garlic cloves,
   finely chopped
2 tsp Worcestershire sauce
3 sheets frozen puff pastry,
   thawed
1 egg, lightly beaten
1 tbs nigella seeds or black
   sesame seeds
Sliced red onion, mint
   leaves and tomato,
   to serve

Preheat oven to 180°C (gas mark 4). Line a large baking tray with baking paper.

Combine lamb, breadcrumbs, mint jelly, chopped mint, haloumi, garlic and Worcestershire sauce in a bowl. Season with sea salt and freshly ground black pepper. Divide mixture into 6 equal portions, then form each into a long sausage.

Cut each pastry sheet in half. Place a sausage lengthways in the centre of a halved sheet. Brush edges of pastry with a little cold water, then roll up pastry around sausage, sealing edges. Cut each length into 4 sausage rolls, then place, sealed side down, on baking tray. Repeat with remaining pastry and sausage mixture. Brush with beaten egg, then sprinkle over seeds.

Bake for 30 minutes or until puffed and golden. Serve warm with onion, mint and tomato. **Makes 24**

PRAWN & PORK GYOZA

125g raw prawn meat
125g pork mince
2 shallots, finely chopped
2 tbs grated ginger
2 tsp sesame oil
2 tsp soy sauce
1/4 tsp caster sugar
1/4 tsp cornflour
24 gow gee gyoza wrappers
80ml peanut (groundnut) oil
2 spring onions, thinly sliced
   on an angle

Gyoza dipping sauce
125ml Chinese black
   (chinkiang) vinegar
2 tbs peanut
   (groundnut) oil
2 tbs finely chopped
   coriander leaves
1 long red chilli, seeds
   removed, chopped
1 tbs grated ginger
1 tsp soy sauce

To make dipping sauce, whisk together all ingredients in a bowl, then set aside until ready to serve.

Line a baking tray with baking paper.

To make gyoza filling, combine all ingredients, except wrappers, peanut oil and spring onion, in a food processor and pulse to just combine (do not overprocess).

Holding a gow gee wrapper in the palm of one hand, place 1 heaped teaspoonful of filling in the centre of the wrapper. Wet edges of wrapper with a little cold water, then fold edges together, crimping edges to seal. Place, crimped edge up, on lined tray. Repeat with remaining wrappers and filling.

Place a large frypan (with a lid) over medium heat and add 1 tbs oil. Place 12 gyoza, crimped edge up, in pan and cook, uncovered, for 3-4 minutes until browned on the base. Add 60ml water to pan, then quickly cover with lid and steam gyoza for 2 minutes or until cooked through. Remove lid, make sure all the gyoza are still sitting crimped edge up, then add another 1 tbs oil to the pan and cook gyoza for a further 1 minute or until bases are crisp. Remove from pan and keep warm, then repeat process with the remaining 12 gyoza and 2 tbs oil.

Transfer gyoza to a serving platter, scatter with spring onion and serve with dipping sauce. **Makes 24**

PROSCIUTTO, QUINCE & PEAR TOASTIES

8 slices woodfired bread
90g quince paste
1 pear, cored, thinly sliced
4 slices prosciutto
200g manchego cheese
  or vintage cheddar,
  grated
1 tsp thyme leaves
2 tbs oil
40g unsalted butter
Mixed bitter leaves (such
  as radicchio, chicory and
  rocket), to serve

Bechamel sauce
25g unsalted butter
2 tbs flour
250ml milk
50g manchego cheese or
  vintage cheddar, grated
Pinch ground nutmeg

To make bechamel, melt butter in a saucepan over medium-low heat. Add flour and cook, stirring, for 2-3 minutes until well combined. Gradually whisk in milk and bring to a simmer, then whisk constantly for 3-4 minutes until thickened. Add cheese and nutmeg, stir until cheese is melted and combined, then season with sea salt and freshly ground black pepper. Cover surface with clingfilm and cool slightly.

Divide quince paste among 4 bread slices, then top each with 1 tbs bechamel. Place 2 pear slices on top of each, then a slice of prosciutto. Divide half the grated cheese among the 4 bread slices, then sprinkle with thyme leaves. Sandwich with remaining 4 bread slices.

Preheat the grill to high.

Heat oil and butter in a frypan over medium-high heat. Cook sandwiches for 1-2 minutes each side until golden. Quickly spread top of each sandwich with remaining bechamel, sprinkle over remaining grated cheese, then grill until golden and bubbling. Serve with mixed bitter leaves. **Makes 4 toasties**

Flex your MUSSELS

SEAFOOD

Vongole
(AKA clams)

CRUMBED WHITING WITH CITRUS SALAD

150g plain flour, seasoned
with sea salt and freshly
ground black pepper
2 eggs, lightly beaten
100g panko breadcrumbs
600g skinless whiting fillets
1 tbs lemon juice
1 tbs white wine vinegar
1 tsp wholegrain mustard
1 tsp chopped lemon thyme
or thyme leaves
125ml extra virgin olive oil
2 oranges, segmented
Small fennel bulb,
thinly sliced
1 small frisee (curly endive)
180g nicoise or other small
black olives
150g mayonnaise (see
Essentials p 68) or
store-bought whole-egg
mayonnaise
Sunflower oil, to deep-fry

Place flour, egg and breadcrumbs in three separate bowls. Dust fish first in flour, then dip in egg, then coat in crumbs. Transfer to a plate and refrigerate until needed.

To make dressing, combine lemon juice, vinegar, mustard and thyme in a bowl, then gradually whisk in olive oil. Season with sea salt and freshly ground black pepper. Set aside. Place orange, fennel, frisee and olives in a bowl and toss to combine. Set aside.

Place mayonnaise in a small bowl and loosen to a drizzling consistency with a little warm water. Set aside.

Half-fill a deep-fryer or large saucepan with sunflower oil and heat to 190°C (gas mark 5) (a cube of bread will turn golden in 30 seconds when the oil is hot enough). Working in batches, gently lower fish into oil and deep-fry for 2-3 minutes until golden.

Add dressing to salad mixture and toss to combine. Serve immediately with fish and mayonnaise for drizzling. **Serves 4**

INDIAN SPICED PRAWNS WITH FRESH COCONUT

2 tbs ghee or vegetable oil

2 tbs panch phoran

12 fresh curry leaves

1 onion, halved, thinly sliced

1 tsp ground turmeric

1 tbs mild curry powder

400g raw prawns, peeled
  (tails intact), deveined

3 long green chillies, seeds
  removed, thinly sliced

250ml coconut milk

100g fresh or frozen grated
  coconut or desiccated
  coconut

Coriander leaves, yoghurt,
  tomato kasundi or mango
  chutney and warm naan
  bread, to serve

This simple, aromatic dish is lovely served as part of an Indian feast. Alternatively, serve the prawns as canapés, each one atop a small piece of naan.

Heat ghee in a frypan over medium heat. Add panch phoran and curry leaves, and cook for 1 minute until fragrant. Add onion and cook, stirring, for 3-4 minutes until softened.

Add turmeric and curry powder, then stir to combine. Add prawns and chilli, stir to coat in spice mixture, then cook for 1-2 minutes until the prawns start to turn pink. Add coconut milk and grated coconut, then cook for a further 3-4 minutes until prawns are just cooked. Scatter with coriander leaves and serve with yoghurt, tomato kasundi and naan. **Serves 4**

SALMON, EGG & DILL PIE

100g basmati or
  long-grain rice
80ml double cream
30g unsalted butter,
  chopped
1 tbs finely chopped dill
1 tbs finely chopped
  flat-leaf parsley leaves
Finely grated zest
  of 1 lemon
375g block frozen puff
  pastry, thawed
300g hot-smoked salmon
  fillets, skin removed,
  flaked
3 eggs, soft-boiled,
  quartered, plus 1 lightly
  beaten egg, to brush

Caper butter sauce
120g unsalted butter,
  chopped
2 tbs baby capers, rinsed
2 tbs chopped dill

To make filling, cook rice in boiling salted water for 8 minutes or until just cooked. Rinse under cold running water, then drain well. Transfer to a bowl with the cream, butter, dill, parsley and lemon zest, then season with sea salt and freshly ground black pepper and stir to combine.

Divide pastry in half and roll out 1 portion to a 25cm x 30cm rectangle. Place on a baking tray lined with baking paper and spread over half the rice mixture. Top with salmon, then soft-boiled egg. Brush pastry edges with water, then spread remaining rice over filling. Roll out remaining pastry to a 25cm x 30cm rectangle, then cut with a lattice cutter (available from kitchenware shops). Place on top of rice mixture, pressing edges to seal. Alternatively, roll out remaining portion of pastry to a 25cm x 30cm rectangle and place over filling, pressing edges to seal. Refrigerate pie for 30 minutes.

Preheat the oven to 180°C (gas mark 4). Brush top of pastry with beaten egg, then bake pie for 25-30 minutes until puffed and golden.

To make caper butter sauce, melt butter, without stirring, in a frypan over low heat, skimming any foam from surface. Remove from heat and stand for 1 minute or until milk solids sink to bottom. Carefully pour liquid clarified butter into a jug, discarding solids. Stir in capers and dill.

Slice pie and serve with the warm caper butter sauce. **Serves 6**

BLACKENED FISH WITH MISO SALAD

60ml sake
60ml mirin
75g white miso paste
55g caster sugar
4 x 200g firm white fish
   fillets (such as ling or cod)
1 tbs sunflower oil
1 nashi pear, thinly sliced
1 carrot, thinly sliced
  into matchsticks
150g mooli, finely shredded
50g micro or baby Asian
   salad leaves or shiso
Black sesame seeds,
   to serve

Miso dressing
1 tbs rice vinegar
1 tbs white miso paste
2 tsp grated ginger
$1/2$ tsp caster sugar
4 tbs sunflower oil
1 tsp sesame oil

Place sake and mirin in a saucepan over medium-high heat. Bring to the boil, then cook for 2-5 minutes until slightly reduced. Reduce heat to low and whisk in miso and sugar, whisking until sugar dissolves. Remove from heat and set aside to cool.

Pat fish dry, then add to marinade and turn to coat. Cover and chill for 4 hours or overnight.

Preheat oven to 200°C (gas mark 6). Line a roasting pan with baking paper.

Heat oil in a frypan over medium-high heat. Drain fish, then cook for 1-2 minutes each side until blackened. Transfer roasting pan and roast for 3-4 minutes or until just cooked.

Meanwhile, to make miso salad, combine nashi, carrot, mooli and leaves in a bowl.

To make miso dressing, whisk all ingredients in a small bowl. Add to salad and toss to combine.

To serve, divide fish among 4 plates, pile miso salad on top and sprinkle with sesame seeds. **Serves 4**

CHILLI SCHOOL PRAWNS WITH YUZU MAYONNAISE

2 tbs Szechuan peppercorns
2 tsp whole black
    peppercorns
500g raw king prawns
75g cornflour, seasoned
    with sea salt and freshly
    ground black pepper
Sunflower oil, to deep-fry
2 tbs olive oil
5cm piece ginger, grated
2 garlic cloves,
    finely chopped
2 long red chillies, seeds
    removed, thinly sliced
2 spring onions, thinly sliced
150g mayonnaise (see
    Essentials, p 68) or
    store-bought whole-egg
    mayonnaise
2 tbs yuzu or lime juice

There are so many interesting types of citrus available these days, including native varieties such as finger lime. While fresh yuzu fruit is a rarity in the UK, this Japanese staple is available year round as bottled juice. It's worth trying for its fresh, tangy fragrance and flavour – a cross between lime and mandarin.

Place all peppercorns and 2 tbs sea salt in a spice grinder or mortar and pestle, then grind to a coarse powder. Set aside.

Dust prawns in cornflour mixture, shaking off excess. Half-fill a deep-fryer or large saucepan with sunflower oil and heat until 190°C (gas mark 5) (a cube of bread will turn golden in 30 seconds when the oil is hot enough). Working in batches, gently lower prawns into oil and cook for 3-4 minutes or until crisp and golden.

Heat olive oil in a frypan over medium-high heat. Add ginger, garlic, chilli and spring onion, and cook, stirring, for 1-2 minutes until fragrant. Add prawns, toss to coat, then remove from heat.

Combine mayonnaise and yuzu juice in a small bowl. Sprinkle prawns with Szechuan salt mixture and serve with yuzu mayonnaise for dipping. **Serves 4**

MAYONNAISE

Combine 300ml grapeseed or sunflower oil with 300ml olive oil in a jug.

Whiz 4 egg yolks and 3 tsp Dijon mustard in a food processor. With the motor running, slowly add oil, drop by drop at first, until the mixture starts to thicken, then pour in a steady stream until thick and emulsified. Add 1 tbs water and the juice of ½ lemon, then season with sea salt and ground white pepper.

BEST EVER CHIPS

Preheat the oven to 180°C (gas mark 4) and set a large wire rack over a baking tray lined with paper towel.

Peel, then cut 1kg floury potatoes (such as King Edward) into 1.5cm-thick chips and pat dry with paper towel.

Half-fill a deep-fryer or large saucepan with sunflower or grapeseed oil and heat to 190°C (gas mark 5) (a cube of bread will turn golden in 30 seconds, when oil is ready).

Deep-fry the chips, in 3 batches, until pale golden. Drain on the rack and cool for 10 minutes.

Reheat the oil and deep-fry the chips, in 3 batches, for a further 7-8 minutes until golden. Spread them in a single layer on an unlined tray, then transfer to the oven until all the chips are cooked.

Toss chips with 40g grated parmesan and 2 tbs finely chopped rosemary, then season with sea salt and freshly ground black pepper. **Serves 4**

MOROCCAN FISH STEW

1 tbs olive oil
1 onion, thinly sliced
2 garlic cloves,
   finely chopped
2 tsp grated ginger
2 tsp ras el hanout
1 cinnamon quill
1 tsp harissa
400g can chopped
   tomatoes
500ml chicken or
   vegetable stock
500g seafood marinara mix,
   drained
400g can chickpeas,
   rinsed, drained
2 tsp honey
20g toasted flaked almonds
Coriander leaves, couscous
   and finely chopped edible
   dried flowers (optional),
   to serve

Heat oil in a large frypan over medium heat. Add onion and cook, stirring, for 1-2 minutes until softened. Stir in garlic and ginger. Add ras el hanout, cinnamon, harissa, tomato and stock, reduce heat to medium-low, then cook for 10 minutes or until slightly reduced. Add marina mix and cook for 5 minutes or until just cooked. Add chickpeas and honey, season with sea salt and freshly ground black pepper, then remove from heat. Sprinkle over flaked almonds and coriander.

Toss the flowers through the couscous, if using, and serve with the fish stew. **Serves 4**

MY MUSSEL CHOWDER

2 potatoes, peeled,
  cut into 2cm pieces
1½ tbs olive oil
1 onion, finely chopped
2 garlic cloves,
  finely chopped
2 bacon rashers,
  finely chopped
1 tsp ras el hanout
1kg pot-ready mussels
250ml white wine
300ml double cream
4 slices quick preserved
  lemon (see Essentials,
  p 116) or 1 store-bought
  preserved lemon quarter,
  flesh and white pith
  discarded, rind
  finely chopped
2 tomatoes, seeds
  removed, finely chopped
10 saffron threads
1 tbs thyme leaves
1 tbs finely chopped
  flat-leaf parsley, plus
  extra leaves to serve

Blanch potato in boiling salted water for 3 minutes. Drain.

Heat oil in a large saucepan over medium heat. Add onion, garlic, bacon and ras el hanout, then cook, stirring, for 3-4 minutes until onion starts to soften. Add mussels and wine, cover with a lid, then cook for 4 minutes or until mussels have opened, discarding any that stay closed. Using a slotted spoon, remove mussels from pan and set aside.

Add potato, cream, preserved lemon rind, tomato, saffron and thyme to sauce and cook for 2-3 minutes until potato is tender. Season with freshly ground black pepper and sea salt (if needed; mussels may be salty enough), then return mussels to pan for 1 minute to warm through.

Sprinkle chowder with chopped parsley and serve scattered with extra parsley leaves. **Serves 4 as a starter or 2 as a main course**

SALMON WITH MEXICAN FLAVOURS

500g tomatoes, seeds
  removed, chopped
2 avocados, quartered
  lengthways, sliced
1 jalapeno, thinly sliced
1 bunch coriander, leaves
  chopped, plus extra
  sprigs to serve
1 small red onion, halved,
  thinly sliced
400g can black turtle beans,
  rinsed, drained
2 tbs lime juice, plus extra
  lime wedges to serve
80ml olive oil
1kg side of salmon or
  ocean trout, skin
  removed, pin-boned
2 tbs brown sugar
2 tbs smoked paprika
1 corn cob
Sour cream, yellow and blue
  corn chips and steamed
  rice, to serve

I love serving a side of salmon when I'm entertaining; it makes such an impressive centrepiece at the shared table. Mexican cooking is also taking centre stage on the culinary scene for feeding a crowd, and its zingy freshness complements the richness of this fish.

Preheat the oven to 120°C (gas mark ½). Line a roasting pan with baking paper.

To make salsa, place tomato, avocado, jalapeno, coriander, onion and black beans in a bowl. Whisk lime juice and 2 tbs oil in a small bowl, season with sea salt and freshly ground black pepper, then set aside.

Place salmon in roasting pan. Combine sugar, paprika and remaining 2 tbs oil in a small bowl, then brush over salmon. Roast for 15-20 minutes until just cooked through, then transfer to a serving platter and pour over cooking juices.

Meanwhile, cook corn in boiling salted water for 5 minutes or until just tender. Drain, refresh under cold running water, then drain again. Cool, then slice kernels from the cob and toss through the tomato mixture with dressing.

Scatter salmon with extra coriander, then serve with salsa, sour cream, corn chips and steamed rice. **Serves 8**

ANTIPASTO FISH PARCELS

4 x 180g skinless white fish
   fillets (such as John Dory)
Olive oil, to drizzle
12 cherry vine tomatoes
50g pitted black olives
1/2 tsp salted capers,
   rinsed, drained
4 marinated artichoke
   hearts, drained
1 roasted red pepper, sliced
150g rinsed, drained
   canned cannellini beans
Juice of 1 lemon, plus extra
   wedges to serve
1 tbs finely chopped
   flat-leaf parsley
Mesclun salad, to serve

Preheat the oven to 200°C (gas mark 6). Cut a sheet of baking paper into four 45cm squares.

Cut each fish fillet into 3 pieces and divide among the baking paper squares, then season with sea salt and freshly ground black pepper and drizzle with oil. Place tomato, olives, capers, artichoke, pepper and beans around fish, then squeeze over the lemon juice. Gather edges of paper and pleat to form parcels, then secure with kitchen string. Place parcels on a baking tray and bake for 10 minutes or until fish is just cooked.

Rest for 5 minutes, then open parcels, sprinkle with parsley and serve with mesclun salad and lemon wedges. **Serves 4**

SPICE-CRUSTED FISH

1 tsp whole black
  peppercorns
1 tbs coriander seeds
1 tsp cumin seeds
2 tsp grated palm sugar
  or brown sugar
2 tbs fried Asian shallots
140g fresh breadcrumbs
3 kaffir lime leaves
2 tbs coriander leaves
Olive oil, for spice paste
4 x 200g firm white fish
  fillets (such as ling
  or mahi mahi)
Coconut cream (optional),
  to drizzle
Thai basil, steamed yellow
  wax and green beans and
  coconut rice (cooked with
  equal parts water and
  coconut milk), to serve

Preheat the oven to 180°C (gas mark 4). To make spice paste, combine peppercorns with coriander and cumin seeds in a small, dry frypan over medium heat and cook, stirring, for 1-2 minutes until fragrant. Transfer to a mortar and pestle or spice grinder and grind to a coarse powder. Place spice mix in a food processor with sugar, shallots, breadcrumbs and kaffir lime and coriander leaves, then pulse until combined. Stir in enough olive oil to form a coarse paste.

Season fish with sea salt and freshly ground black pepper, then place on a roasting pan lined with baking paper. Thickly spread spice paste over the top of the fish, then roast for 10-12 minutes until the topping is crisp and golden, and the fish is just cooked.

Drizzle fish with a little coconut cream, if using, and serve with Thai basil, beans and coconut rice. **Serves 4**

Kitchen string for trussing

Thyme

Poultry shears are a good investment

POULTRY

Make a wish

THAI CHICKEN CURRY FOR SPRING

1¹/₂ tbs sunflower oil

6 shiitake mushrooms

3 garlic cloves,
   finely chopped

¹/₂ quantity green curry
   paste (see Essentials,
   p 92) or 2 tbs
   store-bought paste

250ml chicken stock

400ml coconut milk

500g skinless chicken
   breasts, thinly sliced

100g mangetout,
   halved if large

110g baby green beans,
   trimmed

1 tbs fish sauce

Juice of 1 lime

2 tsp grated palm sugar
   or brown sugar

2 kaffir lime leaves,
   finely shredded

Flat rice noodles or
   steamed rice, to serve

30g picked watercress

100g beansprouts, trimmed

1 tbs coriander leaves

2 spring onions, shredded

1 tbs Thai basil leaves

Edible flowers (such as
   borage, optional)

We tend to think of curries being more suitable for the cooler months, but this spicy green curry is served with a fresh, light salad on top, which makes it a lovely dinner dish for spring and summer, too.

Heat oil in a wok or large frypan, over medium-high heat, add mushrooms and cook for 1-2 minutes until softened. Drain on paper towel. Return pan to the heat, add garlic and curry paste, then cook, stirring, for 1 minute or until fragrant.

Add stock and coconut milk, and bring to a simmer. Add chicken and cook for 2-3 minutes until almost cooked through. Add mangetout and beans, and cook for 1 minute. Add fish sauce, lime juice, sugar and kaffir lime leaves, then return mushrooms to the pan to warm through.

Serve curry with noodles or steamed rice, topped with watercress, beansprouts, coriander, spring onion, Thai basil and edible flowers, if using. **Serves 4**

CRUNCHY CHICKEN WITH TOMATO AND PARMESAN WAFERS

4 x 180g chicken
   breast fillets
100g panko breadcrumbs
1 tbs chopped flat-leaf
   parsley
Finely grated zest
   of 1 lemon
130g grated parmesan
60g unsalted butter,
   melted, cooled
1 tbs olive oil, plus extra
   to shallow-fry
½ bunch rocket
2 large vine-ripened
   tomatoes, sliced
Caramelised balsamic glaze,
   to serve

Cut each chicken breast into 3 lengthways. Using a meat mallet or rolling pin, flatten chicken between two sheets of clingfilm to 1.5cm thick.

Combine crumbs, parsley, lemon zest and 50g parmesan in a shallow bowl and season with sea salt and freshly ground black pepper. Brush chicken all over with butter. Coat chicken in crumbs, shaking over the bowl to remove excess crumbs, then chill to firm up.

Meanwhile, preheat the oven to 180°C (gas mark 4). Line a baking tray with baking paper and place an egg ring or 8cm pastry cutter on the tray. Sprinkle 1 tbs parmesan into ring, then gently lift ring away. Repeat process with remaining cheese to make 8 rounds, leaving room between each to allow for spreading. Bake for 6 minutes or until golden and lacey. Using a palette knife, transfer parmesan wafers to a wire rack to cool.

Heat oil in a frypan over medium-high heat, then cook chicken, in batches, for 2-3 minutes each side until golden, transferring to the oven to keep warm as you cook the remainder.

To serve, layer the tomato, chicken, parmesan crisps and rocket on plates pieces. Drizzle over a little balsamic glaze. **Serves 4**

VELVET CHICKEN WITH SESAME BEAN SALAD

1.5kg whole chicken
160ml rice vinegar
60ml soy sauce
60ml mirin (Japanese
   rice wine)
2 tbs sesame oil
1 tbs grated ginger
2 garlic cloves, thinly sliced
60g brown sugar
2 tbs chopped spring onion,
   plus extra, finely sliced
   on an angle, to serve
300g green beans, trimmed,
   sliced in half on an angle,
   blanched, refreshed
1 tbs toasted sesame seeds

Rinse chicken and pat dry inside and out with paper towel, then truss with kitchen string. Place in a large saucepan, then add enough cold water to cover and 2 tsp sea salt. Bring to the boil over high heat, then reduce heat to low, cover and simmer for 25 minutes. Remove pan from heat and set aside, covered, for 3 hours (the residual heat will continue to gently cook the chicken).

Combine vinegar, soy sauce, mirin, sesame oil, ginger, garlic and sugar in a pan over medium-low heat, stirring until sugar dissolves. Add chopped spring onion, then remove from heat.

Remove chicken from poaching liquid and transfer to a chopping board (strain poaching liquid and freeze for another use, if desired). Remove kitchen string and, using a cleaver or poultry scissors, cut chicken into portions, then place on a platter. Top with beans and extra spring onion, then drizzle over spoonfuls of dressing. Sprinkle with sesame seeds and serve warm or at room temperature with remaining dressing. **Serves 4**

QUAIL UNDER A BRICK WITH ASIAN GREMOLATA

2 oranges

Finely grated zest
and juice of 1 lime

2 spring onions,
finely chopped

60ml soy sauce

60ml rice wine vinegar

60ml mirin

4 garlic cloves,
finely chopped

4 quails, butterflied

2 tsp finely chopped
coriander leaves

35g unsalted peanuts,
finely chopped

Sunflower oil, to brush

2 tbs crushed fried
Asian shallots

This ancient Tuscan method of cooking a whole chicken is called *pollo al mattone*. Weighing it down means that it cooks quickly, resulting in fantastically crisp skin and moist flesh. We've also adapted another Italian classic, gremolata, by using Asian flavourings.

Zest and juice 1 orange and combine with lime zest and juice in a large ziplock bag. Add spring onion, soy sauce, vinegar, mirin and three-quarters of the garlic. Add quails, seal bag and shake gently to coat in marinade. Marinate in the fridge for 3-4 hours.

Meanwhile, for the Asian gremolata, zest remaining orange and combine with remaining garlic, coriander and peanuts in a bowl.

Brush a chargrill or frypan with a little oil and heat over medium heat. Place quails, skin-side down, on chargrill, then place a heavy weight, such as foil-covered bricks or a heavy-based frypan, on top and cook for 3 minutes. Remove weight, turn quails over and replace weight, then cook for a further 2 minutes. Remove quails from pan and rest, loosely covered with foil, for 4 minutes.

Combine fried Asian shallots with gremolata mixture and serve sprinkled over quails. **Serves 4**

MASSAMAN ROAST CHICKEN

1.5kg whole chicken

2 tbs grated ginger

2 kaffir lime leaves,
   finely shredded

2 stalks lemongrass,
   1 grated, 1 cut into thirds

2 limes, 1 halved, 1 juiced

70g Massaman curry paste

1 tbs sunflower oil

500g small new potatoes,
   boiled for 10 minutes,
   drained

250ml chicken stock

400ml coconut milk

2 tsp tamarind puree
   or paste

1 tbs fish sauce

1 tsp grated palm sugar
   or brown sugar

2 tbs chopped unsalted
   peanuts and coriander
   sprigs, to serve

Preheat the oven to 200°C (gas mark 6).

Rinse chicken and pat dry inside and out with paper towel. Place in an oiled roasting pan. Combine half the ginger, half the kaffir lime leaves and the grated lemongrass in a small bowl. Place in chicken cavity with halved lime and remaining 3 pieces of lemongrass. Tie chicken legs with kitchen string.

Combine 1 tbs curry paste with oil. Rub all over the chicken and season. Cover loosely with foil, then roast for 40 minutes. Remove foil, then add potatoes to the pan and baste with pan juices. Roast for a further 40 minutes or until potatoes are tender and juices run clear when the thickest part of the chicken thigh is pierced. Transfer chicken and potatoes to a serving dish, loosely cover with foil and set aside to rest.

Meanwhile, place roasting pan on the stovetop, add remaining ginger and curry paste, and stir over a low heat for 1 minute or until fragrant. Add stock and simmer for 3-4 minutes until reduced by half. Add coconut milk and simmer until reduced and thickened. Add tamarind puree, fish sauce, lime juice and sugar, then stir to combine. Pour around the chicken in the serving dish, or into a jug.

Carve chicken and serve with Massaman gravy, scattered with peanuts, coriander and remaining kaffir lime leaves. **Serves 4**

THAI GREEN CURRY PASTE

Place 4 long green chillies, 2 Asian (red) shallots, 1.5cm piece peeled ginger, 2 garlic cloves, chopped roots and stems of ½ bunch coriander, 2 inner stalks of lemongrass, juice of 1 lime, 8 chopped kaffir lime leaves, 2.5cm piece peeled galangal (or substitute ginger), 1 tbs ground coriander, 1 tsp ground cumin, 1 tsp ground black pepper, 2 tsp fish sauce and 60ml sunflower oil in a food processor or blender and whiz to a paste.

GARLIC BREAD SAUCE

Warm 500ml milk, 2 bay leaves and 2 rosemary sprigs in a saucepan over low heat for 5 minutes. Set aside for flavours to infuse.

Melt 75g unsalted butter in a frypan over low heat, add the chopped white part of 1 leek and 10 thinly sliced garlic cloves and cook, stirring, for 5 minutes or until softened.

Discard bay and rosemary, then add warm milk to the leek mixture.

Add 125g fresh white breadcrumbs and a pinch of nutmeg, and stir to combine. Increase heat and bring to just below boiling point.

Stir in 2 tbs double cream and season with sea salt and freshly ground black pepper.

Transfer mixture to a blender and blend until smooth.

TUNISIAN SPICED CHICKEN WITH HUMMUS AND POMEGRANATE

1 tsp ground ginger

1 tsp mixed spice

1/2 tsp ground turmeric

2 tsp ground cumin

125ml olive oil

4 garlic cloves,
    finely chopped

Juice of 1 lemon, plus extra
    lemon wedges to serve

8 skinless chicken
    thigh fillets

1 small red onion,
    thinly sliced

60g picked watercress

Seeds of 1/2 pomegranate

1/2 tsp sumac

4 warm flatbreads,
    quartered, to serve

350g tub good-quality
    hummus

Combine ginger, mixed spice, turmeric, cumin, garlic, 60ml olive oil and half the lemon juice in a large bowl. Add chicken, turning to coat well. Cover and refrigerate for 1 hour.

Soak onion in a bowl of cold salted water for 15 minutes. Drain, then rinse and pat dry with paper towel. Combine onion, watercress and pomegranate seeds in a bowl, then set aside.

Heat a chargrill or frypan over medium-high heat. Drain chicken, then cook for 4-5 minutes each side until golden and cooked.

Toss salad with sumac, 2 tbs olive oil and remaining lemon juice. Season with sea salt and freshly ground black pepper.

Divide flatbreads among 4 plates and top with hummus, chicken and salad. Drizzle with remaining 1 tbs olive oil and serve with extra lemon wedges. **Serves 4**

CHAR SIU DUCK LEGS WITH ASIAN SLAW

2 tbs each soy sauce, honey
   and rice vinegar
80ml hoisin sauce
1 tbs fish sauce
1 star anise
2 garlic cloves,
   finely chopped
4 duck marylands
   (leg quarters)

Asian slaw
80g shredded Chinese
   cabbage
80g shredded red cabbage
1 cucumber, halved
   lengthways, seeds
   removed, thinly sliced
   on the diagonal
1 carrot, thinly sliced
   into matchsticks
1/2 bunch each mint and
   coriander, leaves picked
1/2 tbs each black and
   white sesame seeds
2 tbs extra virgin olive oil
1 1/2 tbs light soy sauce
1/2 tbs honey
1/2 tbs mirin
Juice of 1/2 lime

Begin this recipe a day ahead.

Combine soy sauce, honey, rice vinegar, hoisin and fish sauces, star anise and garlic in a bowl. Add duck, turning to coat, then cover and marinate in the fridge for at least 4 hours or overnight.

Preheat the oven to 180°C (gas mark 4). Line a roasting pan with foil.

Drain duck, reserving marinade. Roast duck, skin-side up, for 25-30 minutes or until dark, caramelised and cooked through. Loosely cover with foil and set aside to rest for 5 minutes.

Meanwhile, to make Asian slaw, place vegetables, herbs and sesame seeds in a large bowl. Place oil, soy sauce, honey, mirin and lime juice in a small bowl and whisk to combine. Add to vegetable mixture and toss well to combine.

Place duck marinade in a small saucepan over medium heat. Bring to the boil, then reduce heat to medium-low and cook for 2-3 minutes until syrupy, then brush over duck before serving.

Serve duck with Asian slaw. **Serves 4**

ROAST CHICKEN WITH GARLIC BREAD SAUCE

1.5kg whole chicken

60ml olive oil

1 large onion, finely chopped

8 cloves garlic, 2 finely chopped, 6 unpeeled

160g fresh breadcrumbs

2 tbs roughly chopped flat-leaf parsley

Finely grated zest of 1 lemon

3 tsp thyme leaves

625ml chicken stock

1½ tbs plain flour

1 quantity of garlic bread sauce (see Essentials, p 93) and roasted seasonal vegetables, to serve

Preheat the oven to 200°C (gas mark 6).

Rinse chicken and pat dry inside and out with paper towel.

Heat 2 tbs oil in a frypan over medium-high heat. Cook onion for 5 minutes or until softened, add chopped garlic and cook for 1 minute or until fragrant. Transfer to a bowl to cool completely. Once cooled, add breadcrumbs, parsley, zest, thyme and 125ml stock, and combine well. Season with sea salt and freshly ground black pepper. Stuff breadcrumb mixture into chicken cavity, then truss chicken with kitchen string.

Place in a lightly oiled roasting pan with unpeeled garlic cloves, drizzle with remaining 1 tbs oil and season. Roast for 15 minutes, then reduce heat to 180°C (gas mark 4) and roast for 1 hour or until juices run clear when the thickest part of the thigh is pierced. Transfer chicken to a platter, loosely cover with foil and rest for 20 minutes.

Meanwhile, to make gravy, drain fat from roasting pan, leaving 1 tbs fat in pan. Transfer to stovetop over medium heat, add flour and cook, stirring, until slightly browned. Add remaining 500ml stock and cook for 2-3 minutes, stirring constantly, until thickened. Strain into a jug and keep warm.

Serve roast chicken with garlic bread sauce, gravy and roasted seasonal vegetables. **Serves 4**

PAN-FRIED CHICKEN WITH TUSCAN BEANS

4 chicken supremes or
    chicken breast fillets
    (skin on)
3 rosemary sprigs
Finely grated zest
    and juice of 1 lemon
3 tbs finely chopped
    flat-leaf parsley
60ml olive oil
1/2 tsp dried chilli flakes
150g pancetta or speck,
    chopped
1 onion, finely chopped
2 garlic cloves, sliced
2 x 400g cans cannellini
    beans, drained, rinsed
150ml dry white wine
200ml chicken stock
2 tomatoes, seeds
    removed, finely chopped
70g fresh breadcrumbs

Make several slashes in the chicken to allow marinade to soak in. Remove leaves from 1 rosemary sprig and finely chop, then combine with lemon zest and juice, 1 tbs chopped parsley, 2 tbs olive oil and chilli flakes. Season with sea salt and freshly ground black pepper. Coat chicken in the mixture, then cover and marinate in the fridge for at least 30 minutes or up to 12 hours.

Preheat the oven to 200°C (gas mark 6). Place pancetta in a frypan over low heat and cook slowly until starting to crisp and fat is rendered. Transfer to a baking dish. Add onion and garlic to same frypan and cook for 3-4 minutes until softened. Add to the pancetta with the beans, wine, stock, tomato and remaining 2 rosemary sprigs. Bake for 20 minutes.

Meanwhile, heat a large frypan over medium-high heat and cook chicken, skin-side down, for 2-3 minutes until golden. Transfer chicken, skin-side up, to the baking dish on top of bean mixture, then bake for a further 20 minutes or until chicken is just cooked. Remove from oven, loosely cover with foil, then set aside for 5 minutes to rest.

Meanwhile, return frypan to medium-high heat, add remaining 1 tbs oil and fry breadcrumbs, stirring occasionally, until golden brown. Toss through 1 tbs parsley.

Using a fork, roughly mash some of the beans to help thicken the sauce. (If there is still too much liquid, transfer the bean mixture to a saucepan and cook over medium heat until reduced.) Stir the remaining 1 tbs parsley through the beans. Serve the chicken with the beans, scattered with parsley breadcrumbs. **Serves 4**

WASABI CRUMBED CHICKEN

2¹/₂ tbs wasabi paste

4 x 170g skinless chicken
   breast fillets

75g whole-egg mayonnaise

75g wasabi peas

50g panko breadcrumbs

2 tbs cornflour

2 eggs, lightly beaten

Peanut (groundnut) oil,
   to shallow-fry, plus
    1 tbs extra

2 carrots, thinly sliced
   into matchsticks

2 celery stalks, thinly sliced
   into matchsticks

4 radishes, thinly sliced

150g mangetout,
   trimmed, thinly sliced
   into matchsticks

1 tbs soy sauce

1 tbs rice or white
   wine vinegar

Warren Mendes, *delicious.* assistant food editor, came up with this spicy take on chicken kara-age (fried chicken), a moreish Japanese staple. The wasabi peas add an extra hit of heat and crunch to the crumb mix.

Brush 2 tsp wasabi paste over each chicken breast and marinate in the fridge for 20 minutes. Combine the mayonnaise and remaining 2 tsp wasabi paste in a bowl and set aside.

Whiz wasabi peas in a food processor until roughly chopped, add breadcrumbs and pulse to combine. Transfer to a shallow bowl and season. Dust the chicken in the cornflour, shaking off excess, then dip in the egg, then coat in crumb mixture.

Place a large frypan over medium-high heat and add 1cm oil. Shallow-fry chicken for 3 minutes each side or until crisp, golden and cooked through, then drain on paper towel.

Place the carrot, celery, radish and mangetout in a bowl. Whisk the soy sauce, vinegar and extra 1 tbs oil in a bowl, then season and toss with the salad to combine. Slice the chicken and serve with the salad and wasabi mayonnaise. **Serves 4**

Stay sharp!

MEAT

BEEF ROULADES WITH PARSLEY PESTO

25g flat-leaf parsley,
  roughly chopped
50g toasted walnuts
40g grated parmesan
2 garlic cloves, chopped
60ml olive oil,
  plus extra to cook
1kg centre-cut beef
  eye fillet (tenderloin)
5 slices prosciutto
400g cherry vine tomatoes
Rocket leaves, to serve

To make pesto, place parsley, walnuts, parmesan and garlic in a food processer and pulse briefly to combine. Gradually pulse in oil until a coarse paste forms.

Place a large sheet of clingfilm on the benchtop. Cut down the centre of beef lengthways, without cutting all the way through, then open out flat. Using a rolling pin, gently beat out beef to an even thickness. Season with sea salt and freshly ground black pepper, then spread three-quarters of the pesto over the meat. Place prosciutto slices, widthways, over pesto, then roll up beef tightly, tying along its length with kitchen string at 3cm intervals. Tightly wrap in the clingfilm and chill for 2 hours.

Preheat the oven to 200°C (gas mark 6). Remove roulade from fridge and bring to room temperature.

Heat a little extra oil in a large, ovenproof frypan or roasting pan over medium-high heat, then brown roulade, turning, to seal all over. Transfer to oven and roast for 20 minutes for rare or until cooked to your liking. Season tomatoes and add to pan for the last 5 minutes of cooking or until slightly wilted. Cover pan loosely with foil and set aside to rest for 10 minutes.

Thickly slice roulade, drizzle with remaining pesto and serve with roasted tomatoes and rocket.

Serves 4

MEXICAN PULL-APART PORK

2 tbs olive oil

1kg pork shoulder,
   boned, tied

2 red peppers, seeds
   removed, thinly sliced

2 onions, thinly sliced

395g jar pico de gallo salsa
   or other tomato salsa

300ml barbecue sauce

4 garlic cloves,
   finely chopped

2 tsp ground cumin

$1/2$ tsp cayenne

1 tsp dried oregano

12 flour tortillas, sour cream
   and lime wedges,
   to serve

Quick pickle

80ml white wine vinegar

2 tsp caster sugar

$1/2$ red onion, thinly sliced

$1/2$ cucumber, halved
   lengthways, seeds
   removed, thinly sliced

Preheat the oven to 160°C (gas mark 3).

Heat oil in a large casserole over medium-high heat and brown pork all over. Add peppers, onion, salsa, barbecue sauce, garlic, spices and oregano to the casserole and bring to the boil, basting pork in the sauce. Season with sea salt and freshly ground black pepper, then place a sheet of baking paper directly on top of the pork. Cover with a lid and cook in the oven for 3 hours or until meat is very tender.

Meanwhile, to make quick pickle, place vinegar, sugar and 1 tsp sea salt in a bowl and stir until sugar and salt dissolve. Add onion and cucumber, and stir to coat, then marinate in the fridge for 15 minutes.

Remove string from pork and shred meat. Serve with tortillas, quick pickle, sour cream and lime wedges. **Serves 4-6**

MOORISH BEEF SKEWERS WITH CAULIFLOWER COUSCOUS

2 tbs cumin

1 tbs sweet paprika

1/2 tsp smoked paprika

1 tsp nutmeg

1 tsp turmeric

1/2 tsp cayenne

15g flat-leaf parsley, finely
    chopped

2 garlic cloves,
    finely chopped

125ml Pedro Ximénez
    or other sweet sherry

80ml extra virgin olive oil

1.2 kg beef rump,
    cut into 4cm pieces

1 lemon, thickly sliced

Cauliflower couscous

150g couscous

200g cauliflower florets

2 tbs extra virgin olive oil

40g dried cranberries

2 tbs pistachios

1 heaped tsp finely
    chopped flat-leaf parsley

Combine spices, parsley, garlic, sherry and olive oil in a large, non-reactive glass or ceramic bowl. Add beef and turn to coat. Cover and marinate in the fridge for 4 hours.

Soak 8 bamboo skewers in cold water for 30 minutes (or use 8 metal skewers).

Meanwhile, to make cauliflower couscous, place couscous in a bowl and pour over 185ml warm water. Cover with a tea towel and set aside. Cook cauliflower in boiling salted water for 3 minutes or until just tender (don't overcook). Drain and refresh under cold running water. Dry well on paper towel, then place in a food processor and pulse to the consistency of breadcrumbs. Fluff couscous with a fork, season with sea salt and freshly ground black pepper, then stir through cauliflower, olive oil, cranberries, pistachios and parsley.

Drain beef and thread onto skewers. Heat a chargrill pan or barbecue to high. Cook the skewers, turning and brushing occasionally with marinade, for 3-4 minutes until medium-rare or until cooked to your liking. Cook the lemon slices for 1-2 minutes each side until lightly charred.

Serve beef skewers with cauliflower couscous and chargrilled lemon slices. **Serves 4**

STIR-FRIED PORK & BEAN SAMBAL IN LETTUCE CUPS

1 tbs sunflower oil

2 garlic cloves,
    finely chopped

2 small red chillies, seeds
    removed, finely chopped

3 Asian (red) shallots, thinly
    sliced

250g lean pork mince

1 tbs fish sauce

1 tbs oyster sauce

2 tsp Chinese black
    (chinkiang) vinegar

1 tsp kecap manis

100g green beans, trimmed,
    cut into 2cm lengths

1 tbs chilli jam

1 tomato, seeds removed,
    chopped

2 tbs finely chopped
    coriander leaves, plus
    extra leaves to serve

1 butterhead lettuce,
    leaves separated

Steamed rice, to serve

This moreish, spicy sambal is inspired by one I watched chef Christine Manfield make at a cooking demonstration in Tasmania. Her knack for creating layered flavour and texture is amazing.

Heat oil in a wok over high heat. Add garlic, chilli, shallots and pork. Stir-fry for 2 minutes, tossing constantly, until pork is no longer pink. Add fish and oyster sauces, vinegar, kecap manis and beans, and toss to combine. Add chilli jam, tomato and coriander, and stir-fry for a further 1 minute.

To serve, fill lettuce cups with spoonfuls of steamed rice and top with the pork mixture and extra coriander leaves.

Serves 4 as a starter or as part of an Asian banquet

SLOW-COOKED LAMB SHOULDER WITH CHILLI MINT SAUCE

2kg lamb shoulder (bone in)
2 tbs fish sauce
60ml sweet chilli sauce
    (see Essentials, p 45)
    or store-bought sweet
    chilli sauce
1 heaped tsp finely
    chopped mint
1 tbs olive oil
1 quantity of the best
    crunchy potatoes
    (see Essentials, p 117)

Chilli mint sauce
2 tbs grated palm sugar
    or brown sugar
2 tbs peanut oil
60ml rice vinegar
Finely grated zest and juice
    of 1 lime
2 long red chillies,
    thinly sliced
1 red onion, thinly sliced
40g mint leaves

Preheat the oven to 180°C (gas mark 4).

Using the tip of a sharp knife, cut a cross-hatch pattern all over the lamb skin. Combine fish and sweet chilli sauces, chopped mint and 1 tbs oil in a bowl. Place lamb on a rack set in a roasting pan and brush all over with marinade. Fill pan with 2cm hot water, then cover pan with foil. Roast for 1$^1/_2$ hours, then remove foil and roast for a further 45 minutes. Cover loosely with foil and set aside to rest for 15 minutes.

To make chilli mint sauce, place all the ingredients in a bowl and stir until sugar dissolves. Carve lamb and serve with crunchy potatoes and chilli mint sauce. **Serves 4-6**

QUICK PRESERVED LEMONS

Wash 3 organic or unwaxed lemons, then thinly slice.

Combine 75g caster sugar and 75g sea salt.

Layer lemon slices with the salt mixture in a non-reactive glass or ceramic bowl. Cover with clingfilm and set aside at room temperature overnight.

The next day, layer lemons, with their juices, any residual sugar and salt, 2 or 3 bay leaves and 2 tbs coriander seeds in sterilised jars, topping up with extra lemon juice to cover, if necessary.

Store for up to 3 months.
Makes 1 litre

THE BEST CRUNCHY POTATOES

Preheat the oven to 190°C (gas mark 5).

Peel 10 King Edward or Desiree potatoes, cut into
3-4cm pieces and add to a saucepan
of cold salted water.

Bring to the boil over medium-high heat
and boil for 2 minutes.

Drain well, then return potatoes to the saucepan,
shaking it a few times to roughen the edges.

Toss potatoes in 2 tbs plain flour and season
with sea salt and freshly ground black pepper.

Heat 100g duck fat and 2 tbs sunflower oil in
a large, shallow roasting pan for 5 minutes.

Carefully add floured potatoes to the pan
and roast for 20 minutes, then turn using tongs.

Roast for a further 20 minutes, turn again,
then roast for a final 10-15 minutes until
crunchy and golden. **Serves 4-6**

LAMB & PRESERVED LEMON MEATBALLS WITH CRUSHED BROAD BEAN SALAD

35g fresh breadcrumbs

60ml milk

500g lamb mince

1 garlic clove,
    finely chopped

40g grated parmesan

2 tbs finely chopped
    preserved lemon rind
    (see Essentials, p 116)

1 tbs finely chopped mint
    leaves, plus extra leaves
    to serve

500g podded fresh or
    frozen broad beans

1 tsp lemon zest

2 tbs olive oil

Warm flatbreads,
    watercress sprigs,
    Greek-style yoghurt and
    lemon wedges, to serve

Combine breadcrumbs and milk in a bowl. Set aside for 5 minutes.

Place lamb, garlic, parmesan, preserved lemon and half the chopped mint in a bowl. Season well with sea salt and freshly ground black pepper, then add breadcrumb mixture and combine well. Roll lamb mixture into 3cm balls and place on a plate. Cover and refrigerate to firm up.

Cook fresh broad beans in a saucepan of boiling salted water for 3 minutes or blanch frozen broad beans for 1 minute. Drain, refresh in iced water, then remove outer pods. Place beans in a bowl with lemon zest, 1 tbs oil and remaining 1 heaped tsp chopped mint. Season, then roughly crush beans with a fork.

Heat remaining 1 tbs oil in a large frypan over medium-high heat. Cook meatballs, turning, for 4-5 minutes until browned all over and cooked through.

Serve meatballs with flatbread, broad bean salad, watercress, yoghurt, lemon wedges and extra mint leaves. **Serves 4**

PEPOSO WITH PAN-FRIED GNOCCHI

1.5kg beef cheeks
  cut into 2cm pieces
4 garlic cloves,
  finely chopped
1 carrot, cut into
  1cm pieces
2 celery stalks,
  cut into 1cm pieces
1 red onion, cut into
  1cm pieces
1L Chianti or other red wine
1 tbs freshly ground
  black pepper
1 tbs tomato paste
2 bay leaves
500ml veal or beef stock
500g potato gnocchi
20g unsalted butter
2 tbs olive oil
1 tbs finely chopped
  flat-leaf parsley, to serve

This medieval Tuscan 'pepper stew' may have been born of necessity – cheap cuts of meat, often past their best, were cooked for hours with copious amounts of Chianti, pepper and garlic to tenderise them and disguise their dubious flavour. But this version, made with beef cheeks, unctuous and warmly fragrant with pepper, is positively luxurious on a cold winter's night.

Place beef in a large saucepan with garlic, carrot, celery and onion. Pour over enough wine to cover. Bring to the boil over medium-high heat, then reduce heat to low. Cover closely with a round of baking paper (cartouche), then cover pan with a tight-fitting lid and simmer for 2 hours.

Add pepper, tomato paste, bay leaves, stock and remaining wine. Simmer, uncovered, for a further 2 hours (adding a little more stock or water if it starts to dry out) or until beef is very tender. Season well with sea salt.

Cook gnocchi in a large saucepan of boiling salted water until they rise to the surface. Drain well. Heat butter and oil in a large frypan over medium-high heat, then cook gnocchi, turning, for 2-3 minutes until golden and crisp. Serve peposo with pan-fried gnocchi, and garnished with parsley. **Serves 4-6**

CRISP PORK BELLY WITH GREEN PAPAYA SALAD

1 tbs fennel seeds

1 tbs coriander seeds

1 tbs thyme leaves

1kg boneless pork belly
  (skin on)

1 tbs olive oil

Green papaya salad

6 snake beans (yard long
  beans), trimmed,
  cut into 3cm lengths

1/2 green papaya

250g cherry tomatoes,
  quartered

30g Thai basil leaves

30g coriander leaves

2 garlic cloves,
  finely chopped

2 small red chillies, seeds
  removed, finely chopped

50g roasted unsalted
  peanuts

2 tbs grated palm sugar
  or caster sugar

1 tbs rice vinegar

60ml lime juice

60ml fish sauce

Combine fennel seeds, coriander seeds and thyme with 2 tsp sea salt. Rub pork all over with olive oil, then press spice mix into the skin. Refrigerate for 1 hour.

Preheat the oven to 240°C (gas mark 9). Bring pork to room temperature.

Place pork on a rack set in a roasting pan, pour 250ml water into the base of the pan and roast for 30 minutes. Reduce oven to 170°C (gas mark 3) and roast for a further 1 1/2 hours or until skin is crisp and meat is very tender. Cover loosely with foil and set aside to rest for 10 minutes.

Meanwhile, to make salad, blanch beans for 1 minute, drain and refresh in iced water. Drain again and place in a bowl. Using a mandoline or sharp knife, finely shred the papaya, then place in the bowl with the beans, tomato and herbs. Pound garlic and chilli to a paste using a mortar and pestle. Add peanuts and pound to a coarse paste. Add sugar, rice vinegar, lime juice and fish sauce to taste (the mixture should be a balance of sweet, sour, salty and hot flavours) and stir until sugar dissolves. Add dressing to papaya mixture and toss to combine.

Slice the pork and serve with green papaya salad. **Serves 4**

SPICE-CRUSTED LAMB RACKS WITH MOJO POTATOES

125ml olive oil

4 x 4- or 5-bone lamb racks

2 tsp ground cumin

2 tsp dried oregano

2 tsp dried thyme

2 tsp black peppercorns

2 garlic cloves, chopped

Mojo potatoes

1 green pepper,
   seeds removed,
   roughly chopped

1 bunch flat-leaf parsley,
   plus extra sprigs to serve

1/2 long green chilli,
   seeds removed,
   roughly chopped

2 tsp ground cumin

50ml extra virgin olive oil

1 garlic clove

2 thyme sprigs,
   leaves picked

600g waxy potatoes,
   peeled, boiled, cut
   into 2cm pieces

Heat 1 tbs oil in a large ovenproof frypan or roasting pan over medium-high heat and brown lamb racks on both sides. Set aside to cool completely.

Meanwhile, combine spices, garlic and 100ml olive oil with 2 tsp sea salt in a food processor and process to a smooth paste. Rub into the skin side of the cooled lamb, then cover and marinate in the fridge for 1 hour.

Preheat the oven to 200°C (gas mark 6). Bring lamb to room temperature.

Roast lamb for 8 minutes for rare or until cooked to your liking. Cover loosely with foil and set aside to rest for 5 minutes.

Meanwhile to make mojo potatoes, using a food processor, process pepper, parsley, chilli, cumin, oil, garlic and thyme until finely chopped. Transfer to a bowl with the hot potato and toss to combine.

Carve lamb racks and serve with mojo potatoes and garnished with extra parsley sprigs. **Serves 4-6**

NEW WORLD CURRIED SAUSAGES

1 tbs olive oil
12 fresh curry leaves,
    plus extra to fry
1 tsp panch phoran
1 small onion, thinly sliced
1/2 long green chilli, seeds
    removed, finely chopped
2 garlic cloves,
    finely chopped
2 tsp grated ginger
1 tsp sweet paprika
1/2 tsp curry powder
400g can chopped
    tomatoes
1 tsp caster sugar
1 tsp tamarind puree
400g can chickpeas,
    rinsed, drained
1 tbs chopped coriander
12 thin pork or beef
    sausages
Mashed potato, to serve

This is my version of a dish that anyone who grew up in the 'old country' will recognise either with nostalgia or horror! The original was sausages cooked with curry powder, perhaps some Worcestershire sauce and even a little hot English mustard powder. Here, we've given it a suitably multicultural, Mod-Oz feel to give the old dear a new lease of life. But it's still best with mash…

To make curry sauce, heat oil in a frypan over medium heat. Add curry leaves and panch phoran, then cook, stirring, for 1 minute or until fragrant. Add onion and cook until softened but not coloured. Add chilli, garlic and ginger, then cook for a further 1 minute. Add paprika and curry powder, then cook for a further minute. Add tomato, sugar and tamarind, then cook, stirring occasionally, for 10-15 minutes until thickened and the oil starts to separate. Add 250ml water and bring to a simmer, then add chickpeas and coriander, and simmer for a further 5 minutes.

Meanwhile, cook sausages in a frypan over medium-high heat, turning, until browned and cooked through. In the same pan, fry extra curry leaves until crisp, then drain on paper towel.

Serve sausages with mash, sauce and fried curry leaves. **Serves 4**

LUMACHE
(AKA snails)

Solo
r

PASTA, NOODLES & RICE

Fragrant jasmine rice

CALASPARRA RICE
(Perfect for paella)

ORECCHIETTE WITH HOT-SMOKED SALMON, PEAS & BEURRE BLANC SAUCE

400g orecchiette or other
  short dried pasta
80ml white wine
80ml white wine vinegar
2 shallots, finely chopped
175g chilled unsalted
  butter, chopped
120g frozen peas
250g hot-smoked salmon
  or trout fillets, skin
  removed, flaked
2 tbs double cream
2 tbs chopped dill, plus
  extra sprigs to serve

Cook pasta in a saucepan of boiling salted water according to packet instructions. Drain, reserving 60ml cooking liquid.

Meanwhile, to make beurre blanc sauce, place wine, vinegar and shallots in a saucepan over medium-low heat. Cook for 3-4 minutes until liquid is reduced to 1 tbs. Whisking constantly, add the butter, 1 piece at a time, until mixture is thick. Remove from heat and cover to keep warm.

Blanch peas in boiling salted water for 1 minute. Refresh under cold running water, then drain.

Combine pasta with the beurre blanc sauce in a serving bowl, adding a little of the reserved cooking liquid to loosen, if necessary. Add peas, salmon, cream and dill, and gently toss to combine. Serve with the extra sprigs dill. **Serves 4**

WORLD'S EASIEST TOMATO PASTA SAUCE

80ml olive oil

4 garlic cloves,
   finely chopped

1/2 tsp chilli flakes

2 x 400g cans chopped
   tomatoes

1 tsp caster sugar

150g mixed pitted olives

2 tbs finely chopped
   flat-leaf parsley

400g spaghetti, cooked
   according to packet
   instructions, and torn
   basil leaves, to serve

Everyone needs a go-to pasta sauce to throw together from what's in the pantry, whether you're whipping up a weeknight dinner or something for unexpected guests. Another staple I like to have on hand is a jar of homemade pesto to toss through pasta, slick over chicken or fish, or to liven up a dressing. Turn to Essentials on page 140 for my pesto recipe.

Heat oil in a saucepan over medium heat. Add garlic and cook, stirring, for 1 minute or until fragrant. Add chilli, tomato and sugar, stirring until sugar dissolves, then reduce heat to medium-low and cook for 20 minutes or until thickened. Remove from heat.

Season with sea salt and freshly ground black pepper, then stir in olives and parsley. Serve with spaghetti and basil leaves. **Serves 4**

GREEK LAMB WITH ORZO

2 tbs olive oil

500g lamb mince

1 onion, finely chopped

4 garlic cloves,
   finely chopped

2 tsp ground cinnamon

1 tsp dried oregano

1$\frac{1}{2}$ tsp ground cumin

1$\frac{1}{2}$ tsp ground coriander

$\frac{1}{2}$ tsp dried chilli flakes

2 x 400g cans chopped
   tomatoes

500ml beef stock

500g orzo (risoni) pasta

Juice of 1 lemon

100g baby spinach leaves

20g mint, chopped, plus
   extra leaves to serve

25g flat-leaf parsley,
   chopped

40g pitted kalamata olives

100g crumbled feta

Heat 1 tbs oil in a large saucepan over medium-high heat. Add lamb and cook, breaking up lumps with a wooden spoon, for 2-3 minutes until browned. Transfer lamb to a plate, draining the fat, and set aside until needed.

Return saucepan to medium heat with the remaining 1 tbs oil. Add onion and garlic, and cook, stirring, for 5 minutes or until soft. Add spices and dried herbs, season with sea salt and freshly ground black pepper, then cook, stirring, for 1 minute or until fragrant. Add tomato and stock, bring to a simmer, then cook, uncovered, for 25 minutes. Return the mince to the pan and cook for a further 15 minutes or until the sauce is reduced. Remove from heat.

Meanwhile, cook pasta in a saucepan of boiling salted water according to packet instructions. Drain, reserving 125ml cooking liquid, then return pasta to the pan with lemon juice and toss to combine.

Add the spinach to lamb mixture and toss until wilted, then add mint, parsley and pasta, and toss to combine. Add a little of the reserved liquid if the sauce is too dry.

Serve topped with olives, feta and extra mint leaves. **Serves 4-6**

RIGATONI WITH SPICY SAUSAGE SAUCE

1 onion, chopped
1 carrot, chopped
1 celery stalk, chopped
4 garlic cloves, chopped
1 tbs oregano leaves,
   plus extra to serve
1/2 tsp dried chilli flakes
2 tbs olive oil
500g Italian pork sausages,
   casings removed
500g lean pork mince
1 tbs tomato paste
200ml red wine
2 x 400g cans chopped
   tomatoes
1 tbs chopped
   flat-leaf parsley
500g rigatoni or other
   short dried pasta
Shaved parmesan, to serve

Place onion, carrot, celery, garlic, oregano and chilli flakes in a food processor and whiz until finely chopped. Set aside.

Heat oil in a large saucepan over medium-high heat. Add sausage meat and mince, then cook, breaking up lumps with a wooden spoon, for 3-4 minutes until browned. Remove with a slotted spoon and set aside.

Add vegetable mixture to pan and cook, stirring, for 2-3 minutes until starting to soften. Add tomato paste and cook for 1 minute. Stir in the wine, then return meat to pan with the tomato and parsley. Bring to a simmer, then cook, partially covered, stirring occasionally, for 1 hour or until reduced. Remove from heat.

Meanwhile, cook pasta in a saucepan of boiling salted water according to packet instructions. Drain, reserving 125ml cooking liquid.

Add pasta to sauce and toss to combine, adding a little reserved cooking liquid to loosen the sauce, if necessary. Season with sea salt and freshly ground black pepper, and serve with shaved parmesan and extra oregano. **Serves 4-6**

THREE-CHEESE & MUSHROOM LASAGNE

20g dried porcini
    mushrooms
2 tbs olive oil
2 large onions,
    halved, sliced
1 bay leaf
4 sprigs thyme
800g mixed mushrooms
    (such as shiitake,
    chestnut, brown and
    oyster), sliced if large
4 garlic cloves,
    finely chopped
600ml jar tomato passata
200g mozzarella, sliced
70g butter
40g flour
850ml milk
1/4 tsp ground nutmeg
250g Taleggio cheese,
    rind removed, cut into
    small pieces
300g fresh lasagne sheets
    (see Essentials, p 141)
25g grated parmesan
1 tbs finely chopped
    flat-leaf parsley

Soak porcini in 80ml boiling water for 30 minutes.

Heat oil in a large frypan over medium-high heat. Add onion and cook, stirring, for 4-5 minutes until softened. Add bay leaf, thyme, 500g mushrooms and half the garlic, then cook for 3-4 minutes until the mushrooms are softened and liquid has evaporated. Add passata and porcini with soaking liquid. Bring to the boil, then reduce heat to medium and cook for 5 minutes or until slightly thickened. Season with sea salt and freshly ground black pepper, then remove from heat.

Preheat the oven to 180°C (gas mark 4). To make cheese sauce, melt 40g butter in a saucepan over low heat. Add flour and cook, stirring, for 1-2 minutes until pale golden. Whisking constantly, add milk until smooth, then cook for 2-3 minutes until thickened. Stir in nutmeg and season, then add Taleggio, 1 piece at a time, whisking until melted and combined.

Grease a 2L baking dish. Cover base with lasagne sheets, then top with half the mushroom filling and half the mozzarella. Repeat process, finishing with a layer of lasagne sheets. Pour over cheese sauce. Cover dish with a sheet of baking paper, then foil. Bake for 30 minutes, remove foil and paper, sprinkle over parmesan and bake for a further 15 minutes until golden. Cool for 10 minutes.

Meanwhile, melt remaining 30g butter in a frypan over high heat. Add remaining 300g mushrooms and garlic, then cook, stirring, for 3-4 minutes until softened. Stir in remaining parsley, then scatter mushroom mixture over top of lasagne to serve. **Serves 8**

PESTO

Process 50g toasted pine nuts, 60g basil leaves, 2 garlic cloves and 60g grated parmesan in a food processor until finely chopped.

With the motor running, slowly add 125ml olive oil to form a coarse paste. Season with sea salt and freshly ground black pepper.

Transfer to a sterilised jar and pour over a little extra oil to form a seal before closing with a lid. Store in the fridge for up to 5 days.

PASTA DOUGH

Place 500g '00' flour (super-fine Italian pasta flour) or strong plain flour in a mound on a clean surface and make a well in the centre.

Add 5 whisked eggs, 2 tbs extra virgin olive oil and 1 tsp sea salt to the well. Gradually incorporate the flour into the egg mixture with a gentle flicking motion until the mixture just comes together.

Dust the surface with flour, then knead dough for 5 minutes or until smooth.

Form into a ball, enclose in clingfilm and rest at room temperature for 30 minutes before rolling through a pasta machine.

SIMPLE PAELLA

1 x 1.5kg chicken,
  cut into 8 pieces
1 tbs olive oil
200g dried chorizo, sliced
1 onion, chopped
400g Calasparra or
  medium-grain rice
2 tomatoes, seeds
  removed, chopped
3 garlic cloves, chopped
2 tsp smoked paprika
  (pimenton)
Pinch saffron threads,
  soaked in 60ml water
  for 20 minutes
750ml chicken stock
165ml white wine
60g frozen peas, defrosted
100g store-bought roasted
  pepper, sliced
Chopped flat-leaf parsley
  and lemon wedges
  (optional), to serve

Pat chicken dry with paper towel and season with sea salt and freshly ground black pepper.

Heat oil in a large paella pan or frypan over medium-high heat. Cook chicken, in 2 batches, skin-side down first, for 4 minutes or until browned. Turn over and cook for a further 1 minute. Remove from pan and set aside.

Add chorizo and onion to pan and cook, stirring occasionally, for 2-3 minutes or until golden. Add rice and stir to coat well. Add tomato, garlic, paprika, saffron mixture, stock and wine, and stir to combine. Return chicken to pan and bring to a simmer. Reduce heat to low and cook, stirring occasionally, for 20 minutes or until liquid is almost evaporated and chicken just cooked through.

Stir in peas and pepper, remove from heat, then cover with a lid and rest for 5 minutes. Sprinkle with parsley and serve with lemon wedges, if using. **Serves 4**

SALMON MISO NOODLE SOUP

1 tsp grated ginger

1 tbs mirin

1 tbs soy sauce

60ml fish sauce

2 x 200g skinless salmon
   fillets, pin-boned,
   cut into bite-size pieces

4 sachets miso soup

1 garlic clove,
   finely chopped

100g shiitake mushrooms

1 carrot, cut into
   matchsticks

100g mangetout, trimmed

200g soba noodles

Micro herbs (optional),
   to serve

Combine ginger, mirin, soy sauce and 1 tbs fish sauce in a bowl. Add salmon, turn to coat, then cover and marinate in the fridge for 30 minutes. Drain.

Place miso, remaining 2 tbs fish sauce, garlic and 1L water in a large saucepan over medium-high heat. Bring to a simmer, then add mushrooms and cook for 2-3 minutes until softened. Add carrot, mangetout and salmon, then cook for a further 2 minutes or until salmon is just cooked.

Meanwhile, cook noodles according to packet instructions. Drain, refresh under cold running water, then drain again.

To serve, divide noodles among 4 bowls, pour over soup and scatter with micro herbs, if using. **Serves 4**

GARLICKY PUMPKIN RISOTTO

400g pumpkin, peeled,
  seeds removed, chopped
2 tbs olive oil, plus extra
  to shallow-fry
1.5L vegetable stock
8g unsalted butter,
  chopped
4 garlic cloves,
  finely chopped
1 onion, finely chopped
440g arborio rice
100g parmesan
2 tbs mascarpone
50g shallots, sliced
110g plain flour, seasoned
  with salt and pepper
Sunflower oil, to shallow-fry
1/2 quantity pesto (see
  Essentials, p 116),
  combined with 1 tbs olive
  oil, to serve

Preheat the oven to 180°C (gas mark 4). Place pumpkin in a roasting pan and drizzle with 1 tbs oil. Season with sea salt and freshly ground black pepper, then roast for 20 minutes or until softened.

Bring stock to the boil in a large saucepan, then reduce heat to low and keep at a gentle simmer.

Melt butter and remaining 1 tbs oil in a frypan over medium heat. Add garlic and onion, and cook, stirring, for 1-2 minutes until softened. Add rice and stir for 2 minutes until well coated. Add hot stock, 250ml at a time, stirring constantly, allowing stock to be absorbed before adding the next, until all stock is used, the rice is al dente and the mixture is thick (this will take about 20 minutes). The rice should be creamy but still retain some bite. Gently fold through parmesan, mascarpone and pumpkin. Cover and set aside for 5 minutes.

Meanwhile, heat 2cm sunflower oil in a frypan over high heat. Coat shallots in seasoned flour, shaking off excess, then cook for 1 minute or until golden and crisp.

Serve risotto drizzled with pesto mixture and scattered with crisp fried shallots. **Serves 6**

BLOODY MARY CRAB PASTA

2 tbs olive oil,
1 onion, finely chopped
1 celery stalk, finely
   chopped, plus extra stalks
   to serve
2 garlic cloves,
   finely chopped
2 x 400g cans chopped
   tomatoes
100g unsalted butter,
   chopped
70g sourdough
   breadcrumbs
1 tbs finely chopped
   flat-leaf parsley leaves
2 tsp grated lemon zest
500g spaghetti or other
   dried long pasta
125ml vodka
400g cooked picked
   crabmeat
2 tbs double cream

Here, I've used some of the elements of one of my favourite drinks, a Bloody Mary, and incorporated them into the most delicious pasta dish with crab. The key is to allow the pasta to soak up the vodka before tossing it with the tomato sauce. Oh, and don't forget the classic celery stick on the side.

Heat 1 tbs oil in a saucepan over medium-low heat. Add onion, celery and a good pinch of sea salt, then cook, stirring occasionally, for 5 minutes or until softened. Add garlic, tomato and 125ml water, increase heat to medium and bring to a simmer. Cook for 10-12 minutes until slightly thickened and reduced.

To make parsley crumbs, melt 20g butter and remaining 1 tbs oil in a frypan over medium-high heat. Add breadcrumbs and cook, tossing occasionally, for 2-3 minutes until golden and crisp. Remove from heat and stir through parsley and lemon zest.

Cook pasta in a saucepan of boiling salted water according to packet instructions. Drain, then return pasta to the pan. Add vodka and remaining 80g butter, then stir until melted and combined. Remove from heat.

Add crabmeat and cream to tomato sauce and cook for 1 minute or until warmed through. Add to pasta and toss to combine. Divide pasta among bowls and top with parsley crumbs, and serve with an extra celery stalk. **Serves 6**

SECRET INGREDIENT BOLOGNESE SAUCE

1 carrot, chopped

1 onion, chopped

1 celery stalk, chopped

6 thin slices pancetta, chopped

2 tbs rosemary leaves

2 garlic cloves, chopped

1 tbs olive oil

500g beef mince

1 tbs tomato paste

250ml red wine

400g can chopped tomatoes

250ml tomato passata

250ml beef stock

1 small red chilli, seeds removed, finely chopped

30g dark chocolate (70% cocoa solids), grated

500g tagliatelle or other long dried pasta

Grated parmesan and basil leaves, to serve

Dark chocolate has long played a part in Latin American cooking, its smooth, savoury bitterness lending itself well to meat, poultry and game. Here, it adds an extra dimension of richness to this dinnertime classic.

Place carrot, onion, celery, pancetta, rosemary and garlic in a food processor and process until finely chopped.

Heat oil in a large saucepan over medium-high heat. Add vegetable mixture and cook, stirring, for 5 minutes or until softened. Add mince and cook, breaking up lumps with a wooden spoon, for 3-4 minutes until browned. Add tomato paste and cook for 1 minute, then add wine and cook for 5 minutes or until liquid is reduced by half. Add canned tomato, passata and stock, then season with sea salt and freshly ground black pepper. Cover, reduce heat to low, then cook for 1 hour. Remove lid and cook for a further 30 minutes or until reduced and thickened. Add chilli for the last 5 minutes of cooking. Remove saucepan from heat, add chocolate and stir to combine.

Meanwhile, cook pasta in a large saucepan of boiling salted water according to packet instructions. Drain, then add to sauce and toss to combine. Serve topped with grated parmesan and basil. **Serves 6**

Heirloom carrots

VEGETABLES

Use broccoli leaves in stir-fries

Borlotti beans

Kohlrabi

BEET BURGERS

30g unsalted butter

200g raw beetroot,
    coarsely grated

1 onion, grated

1 tbs red wine vinegar

300g mashed potato

1 tbs sour cream,
    plus extra to serve

1 tsp bottled horseradish,
    plus extra to serve

Sunflower oil, to shallow-fry

Plain flour, to dust

4 burger buns, toasted

Sliced tomatoes, mangetout
    sprouts, sliced avocado,
    sliced red onion and salad
    leaves, to serve

These vegetarian burgers taste just as good as the beef variety, and mini versions make great sliders served in miniature brioche buns for a cocktail party.

Melt butter in a frypan over low heat, add beetroot, onion and vinegar, and cook, stirring, for 10 minutes or until softened. Combine in a bowl with mashed potato, sour cream and horseradish, then season with sea salt and freshly ground black pepper. Form into 4 round patties, then refrigerate for 20 minutes to firm up.

Heat 1cm oil in a frypan over medium-high heat. Dust beetroot patties all over with a little flour, then cook for 2 minutes each side or until golden. Serve in a toasted burger bun with tomato, mangetout, sprouts, avocado, red onion and salad leaves, topped with extra sour cream and horseradish. **Makes 4**

ASPARAGUS WITH CRUMBED HALOUMI

1 tbs honey

1 tsp Dijon mustard

2 tbs cider vinegar

80ml extra virgin olive oil

300g asparagus, trimmed, chargrilled or blanched

3 oranges, peeled, segmented

25g wild rocket

75g plain flour, seasoned with sea salt and freshly ground black pepper

2 eggs, lightly beaten

50g panko breadcrumbs

20g grated parmesan

300g haloumi, drained, thickly sliced into triangles

Olive oil, to shallow-fry

Sprigs of fresh herbs (such as tarragon) to garnish

Whisk together honey, mustard, vinegar and extra virgin olive oil in a bowl.

Combine asparagus, orange and rocket in a bowl.

Place flour and egg in separate bowls. Combine breadcrumbs and parmesan in a third bowl. Dust haloumi first in flour, shaking off excess, then dip in egg, then breadcrumb mixture. Refrigerate for 15 minutes to firm up.

Heat 1cm olive oil in a large frypan over medium-high heat and fry haloumi, in batches if necessary, for 1 minute each side or until crisp and golden.

To serve, add dressing to salad, toss to combine and top with crumbed haloumi and fresh herbs. **Serves 4**

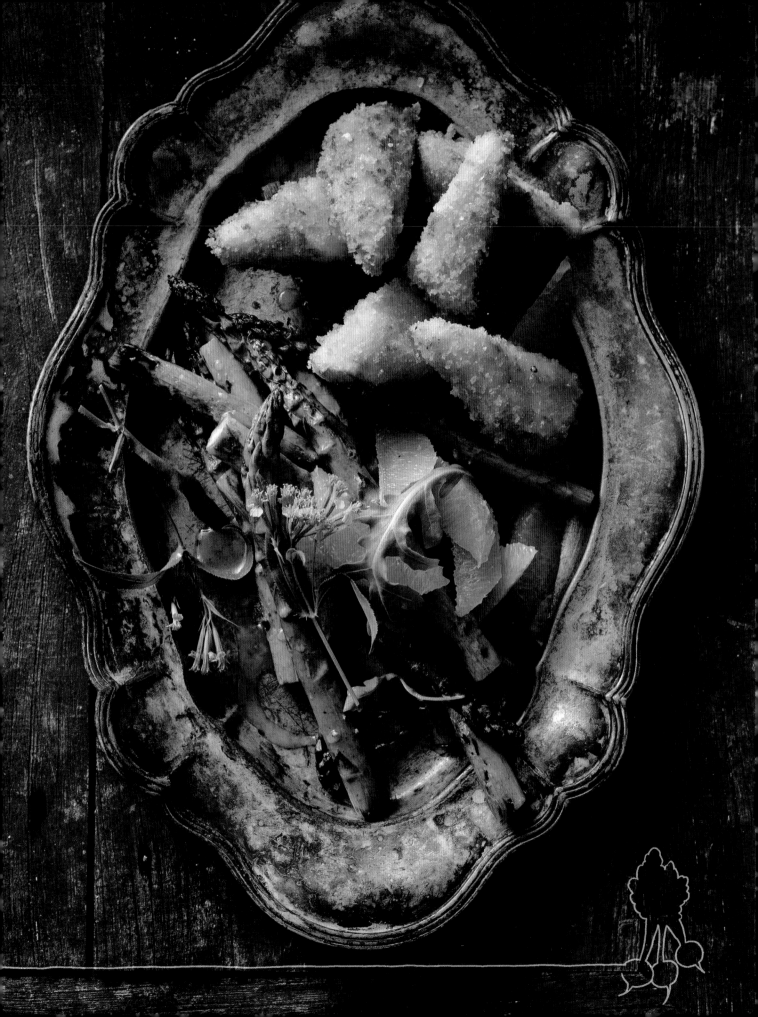

SPICED VEGETABLE COUSCOUS

300g peeled pumpkin,
  seeds removed,
  cut into 3cm pieces
1 carrot, halved lengthways,
  thickly sliced
1 courgette, thickly sliced
1 red onion, cut
  into wedges
1 tbs ras el hanout,
  plus extra to serve
80ml olive oil
250g cherry tomatoes,
  halved
400g can chickpeas,
  rinsed, drained
200g couscous
250ml hot vegetable stock
Finely grated zest and juice
  of 1 lemon, plus wedges
  to serve
2 tsp mint leaves, torn
1 tbs coriander leaves, torn
Tzatziki and pomegranate
  seeds (optional), to serve

Preheat the oven to 200°C (gas mark 6).

Place pumpkin, carrot, courgette and onion in a roasting pan and toss with ras el hanout and 2 tbs oil. Roast for 20 minutes.

Add tomato and chickpeas, and roast for a further 5 minutes or until vegetables are tender and chickpeas are warmed through.

Place couscous in a large bowl. Add stock, cover with a clean tea towel and stand for 10 minutes. Fluff with a fork.

Whisk the lemon juice and remaining 2 tbs oil, then stir through the couscous. Transfer couscous to a platter and top with roasted vegetable mixture.

Just before serving, top with mint and coriander, drizzle over a little tzatziki, and sprinkle over a little extra ras el hanout. Serve with lemon wedges, remaining tzatziki and pomegranate seeds, if using. **Serves 4**

NEW-LOOK COURGETTE SLICE

2 tbs olive oil

1 onion, finely chopped

2 garlic cloves,
    finely chopped

Finely grated zest
    of 1 lemon

2 tbs finely chopped
    coriander leaves

1/4 tsp chilli flakes

6 eggs

35g self-raising flour

500g courgette, grated

1 carrot, grated

120g grated cheddar

2 tbs toasted pine nuts

4 crusty bread rolls, Asian
    salad leaves, mint leaves,
    chilli sauce (optional) and
    sliced long red chillies,
    to serve

We've given the eternally popular courgette slice
a contemporary makeover by serving it banh mi
style, with Asian salad leaves, coriander and chilli.

Preheat the oven to 180°C (gas mark 4). Grease and line a 22cm square cake pan with baking paper.

Heat oil in a frypan over medium-low heat. Cook the onion for 2 minutes or until softened. Add garlic, lemon zest, coriander and chilli, and cook for 2 minutes. Cool slightly.

Meanwhile, whisk together eggs and flour in a large bowl, then season well with sea salt and freshly ground black pepper.

Using a piece of muslin or a J cloth, squeeze out excess moisture from the courgette and carrot. Add to egg mixture with the cooled onion mixture, then stir through grated cheddar. Pour mixture into prepared pan and scatter over pine nuts. Bake for 35-40 minutes until set and pale golden.

Cut courgette slice into long wedges and place in rolls with Asian leaves, mint leaves, chilli sauce, if using, and sliced red chillies. **Serves 4**

HEIRLOOM TOMATO TART

1 quantity of quick puff
  pastry (see Essentials,
  p 165) or 375g block
  frozen puff pastry,
  thawed
480g fresh ricotta, drained
2 eggs, plus 1 egg yolk,
  lightly beaten
60ml double cream
20g grated parmesan
30g grated gruyere cheese
1kg assorted heirloom
  tomatoes, sliced or
  halved if small
1 tbs basil leaves, to serve

Preheat the oven to 180°C (gas mark 4). Line a baking tray with baking paper.

Roll out pastry on a lightly floured surface to a 35cm round. Transfer to lined baking tray.

Combine ricotta, eggs, cream and cheeses in a bowl and season well with sea salt and freshly ground black pepper. Spread ricotta mixture over the pastry round, leaving a 5cm border. Fold in the pastry border over the filling, pleating as you go. Brush the edges of the tart with egg yolk, then bake for 25-30 minutes until golden. Pile tomato slices over tart, season, then scatter over basil leaves. Serve warm or at room temperature. **Serves 4-6**

ONION MARMALADE

Heat 2 tbs olive oil in a large frypan over medium-low heat. Add 600g thinly sliced red or brown onions and a good pinch of sea salt.

Cook, stirring occasionally, for 20-25 minutes until onion has softened and is lightly caramelised.

Add 2 tbs brown sugar, 2 tbs balsamic vinegar and 125ml water, then cook, stirring occasionally, for a further 6-8 minutes until mixture is thick and jammy.

Cool, transfer to a sterilised jar and refrigerate for up to 2 weeks.

QUICK PUFF PASTRY

Sift 250g plain flour into a large bowl with 1 tsp sea salt.

Rub in 250g chilled, chopped unsalted butter until just combined – there should still be large lumps of butter visible in the mixture.

Using a fork, stir in 125ml iced water to form a rough clump of dough.

Transfer the dough to a lightly floured surface and bring the dough together using your hands, then roll out to a rough 20cm x 40cm rectangle.

Fold in one end to the centre, then the other end over the top, then turn dough 90 degrees and roll out again to the same size rectangle. Repeat this process 5 more times until there are no more streaks of butter and the dough is smooth.

Enclose in clingfilm and chill for 30 minutes before using. Or freeze for up to 3 months.

MY PISSALADIERE

2 ficelles or 1 baguette,
  halved
50g unsalted butter,
  melted, cooled
1 quantity onion marmalade
  (see Essentials, p 164)
6 anchovy fillets in oil,
  drained, halved
  lengthways
18 niçoise or other small
  black olives
1 tbs chopped thyme leaves
Extra virgin olive oil,
  to drizzle
Shaved parmesan and torn
  red radicchio (optional),
  to serve

This is a cheat's version of a classic Provençal dish and makes for a great lunch or snack on the run. The onion marmalade is delicious as a relish for sausages, roasted and cold meats, or served with a cheese platter.

Preheat the oven to 180°C (gas mark 4).

Cut along each ficelle lengthways approximately 2cm from top. Remove bread along the centre to make a hollow (reserve tops and bread for breadcrumbs). Scrunch up foil to create a stable base for the ficelles and place on a baking tray. Generously brush inside and outside of ficelles with melted butter, then place, cut-side up, on foil.

Divide onion marmalade between the ficelles, then arrange anchovies over the top in a criss-cross pattern. Scatter over olives and thyme, drizzle with a little extra virgin olive oil and bake for 20-25 minutes until bread is crisp and golden.

Serve topped with shaved parmesan and radicchio, if using.

Serves 2 for lunch or 4 for a snack

MANGO & TOMATO CURRY

2 tbs sunflower oil

1 tbs panch phoran

2 tbs mild curry powder

2 tsp turmeric

4 cardamom pods, bruised

1$^{1}/_{2}$ tbs grated ginger

1 long green chilli, seeds
   removed, finely chopped

10 curry leaves

2 garlic cloves,
   finely chopped

1 onion, halved, sliced

2 mangoes, cut into
   bite-size pieces

6 tomatoes, seeds
   removed, cut into wedges

400ml coconut milk

Steamed rice, chopped
   unsalted roasted peanuts
   and coriander leaves,
   to serve

In Asian curries, tropical fruits are often used in place of, or alongside, meat and vegetables. In this super-quick stir-fry, the mangoes add a rich sweetness to the dish. Perfect for a meat-free Monday dinner, or as part of an Indian banquet.

Heat oil in a wok or large frying pan over medium-high heat. Add spices, ginger, chilli and curry leaves, and stir-fry for 1-2 minutes until fragrant. Add garlic and onion, and stir-fry for a further 2-3 minutes until soft but not browned. Add mango, tomato and coconut milk, and stir-fry until warmed through. Season with sea salt.

   Serve curry with steamed rice, scattered with peanuts and coriander. **Serves 4**

POTATO & PARSNIP CROQUETTES WITH GREEN GODDESS DRESSING

500g Desiree potatoes,
  peeled, chopped
1 large parsnip, chopped
25g unsalted butter
2 tbs finely chopped
  flat-leaf parsley leaves
2 tbs plain flour
2 eggs, lightly whisked
100g panko breadcrumbs
Sunflower oil, to deep-fry
2 baby cos lettuce hearts,
  halved, or salad leaves
  to serve

Green goddess dressing
100g mayonnaise (see
  Essentials, p 68) or
  store-bought whole-egg
  mayonnaise
70g natural or thick
  Greek-style yoghurt
Handful each flat-leaf
  parsley and mint leaves
1/2 bunch chives
2 spring onions (white part
  only), chopped
Juice of 1/2 lime

I'm a huge fan of green goddess dressing. It works a treat in salads and as a dipping sauce for raw vegetables – or wicked crunchy fried ones, such as these.

Place potato and parsnip in a saucepan of cold salted water. Bring to the boil over medium-high heat, then reduce heat to low and simmer for 12-15 minutes until tender. Drain well, add butter, season with sea salt and freshly ground black pepper, then, using a potato ricer or masher, mash until smooth. Stir in parsley, then cover and refrigerate until cold.

Place flour, egg and breadcrumbs in 3 separate bowls. Divide potato mixture into 8 portions and form into croquettes. Dust first in flour, shaking off excess, then dip in egg, then breadcrumbs. Refrigerate for 15 minutes to firm up.

Meanwhile, to make green goddess dressing, whiz all the ingredients in a small food processor until smooth. Season.

Half-fill a deep-fryer or large saucepan with oil and heat to 190°C (gas mark 5) (a cube of bread will turn golden in 30 seconds when the oil is hot enough). Deep-fry croquettes, in batches, for 2-3 minutes until crisp and golden. Keep warm while cooking remainder.

Serve croquettes with cos lettuce hearts and green goddess dressing for dipping. **Makes 8**

ROASTED CARROTS WITH HARISSA MAYONNAISE & DUKKAH

2 bunches heirloom carrots
(assorted, if possible),
scrubbed
1½ tbs olive oil
2 tsp cumin seeds
25g softened unsalted
butter
½ quantity of mayonnaise
(see Essentials, p 68) or
store-bought whole-egg
mayonnaise
2 tsp harissa (or to taste)
Juice of 1 lemon
45g dukkah

Preheat the oven to 180°C (gas mark 4). Line a baking tray with baking paper.

Place carrots on baking tray and drizzle with oil. Scatter with cumin seeds, then dot with the butter. Season with sea salt and freshly ground pepper, then roast, turning once, for 40-45 minutes until tender.

Meanwhile, combine mayonnaise, harissa and 1 tbs lemon juice in a bowl. Place dukkah in a separate small bowl.

Transfer carrots to a platter and drizzle with more lemon juice, then scatter over a little of the dukkah. Serve with bowls of harissa mayonnaise and remaining dukkah for dipping. **Serves 4 as part of a mezze selection**

GRILLED COURGETTE WRAPS

2 tbs olive oil

2 garlic cloves,
  finely chopped

2 long courgettes, trimmed,
  quartered lengthways

160g podded fresh or
  frozen (120g) peas

80g marinated feta, drained

70g thick Greek-style
  yoghurt

2 spring onions, finely
  chopped, plus extra
  thinly sliced on an
  angle to serve

Finely grated zest and juice
  of 1 lemon

4 butterhead lettuce leaves

4 flour tortillas,
  lightly chargrilled

2 tsp mint leaves

1 long red chilli, seeds
  removed, finely shredded

I watched British chef Allegra McEvedy demonstrate this on TV and it looked like such a wonderful, fresh dish for a barbecue that I had to invent my own version.

Combine olive oil and garlic in a bowl. Brush courgette all over with garlic oil and season with sea salt and freshly ground black pepper.

Preheat a chargrill over high heat. Add courgette, flesh-side down, then cover loosely with foil and cook for 3 minutes or until lightly charred. Turn and cook the other flesh side for a further 3 minutes or until lightly charred (don't cook the skin side, as it will burn).

Meanwhile, cook peas in a saucepan of boiling salted water for 3 minutes for fresh and 2 minutes for frozen. Drain, set aside one-third of the peas, then roughly crush the remainder with a fork.

Combine crushed peas with the drained feta and yoghurt in a bowl. Add spring onion, lemon zest and lemon juice, to taste, then season well.

To serve, place a lettuce leaf on each tortilla, top with pea mixture, then place 2 wedges of courgette on top. Scatter with reserved peas, mint leaves, chilli and extra spring onion, then roll up tightly to eat. **Serves 4 as a side**

Radicchio

Baby cos LETTUCE →

Butter LETTUCE

Green Coral LETTUCE ↗

SALADS

Micro cress →

SLOW-ROASTED TOMATOES WITH MOZZARELLA AND SALAMI PANGRATTATO

6 vine-ripened tomatoes

1 tbs olive oil, plus extra
    to drizzle

1 tbs fennel seeds

50g Italian salami,
    roughly chopped

100g sourdough, crusts
    removed, torn into
    small pieces

1 garlic clove,
    finely chopped

2 tbs chopped basil leaves

12 slices prosciutto

2 buffalo mozzarella balls

Wild rocket and pesto
    (see Essentials, p 140),
    to serve

Pangrattato (literally, 'crumb') is often used to finish a pasta dish instead of parmesan. A southern Italian staple, it's known as 'poor man's parmesan', but when combined with lemon zest, herbs or, as we've done here, garlic and salami, it adds a big hit of flavour and texture. Try it with plain pasta that's been tossed with extra virgin olive oil. Delicious.

Preheat the oven to 120°C (gas mark 1/2).

Halve the tomatoes and place, cut-side up, on a baking tray. Drizzle with olive oil, season with sea salt and freshly ground black pepper and sprinkle with fennel seeds. Roast for 2 hours or until tomatoes start to collapse. Set aside to cool slightly.

Meanwhile, heat the oil in a frypan over medium heat, add the salami and cook, turning, until starting to crisp. Drain on paper towel. Add the bread to the same pan and cook, stirring occasionally, for 5 minutes or until golden. Cool slightly, then transfer to a food processor with the salami, garlic and basil, and pulse to crumbs.

Divide tomatoes among 4 plates and top with prosciutto, torn mozzarella and rocket. Drizzle with pesto, then serve scattered with salami pangrattato and drizzled with extra olive oil. **Serves 4**

SALAD OF TOASTED SESAME RICE, SOY BEANS & MUSHROOMS

1¼ tbs sesame oil

200g basmati rice

100g frozen podded soy
  beans, blanched, drained

2 tbs olive oil

1 leek (white part only),
  halved lengthways,
  thinly sliced

1 celery stalk,
  finely chopped

100g shiitake
  mushrooms, sliced

2 spring onions,
  thinly sliced on an angle

1 tbs linseeds (flaxseeds)

1¼ tbs toasted
  sesame seeds

1 tbs light soy sauce

Juice of ½ lemon

½ tsp caster sugar

Heat 1 tbs sesame oil in a saucepan over medium heat. Add half the rice and cook, stirring, for 5 minutes or until toasted. Add remaining rice and 650ml cold water. Bring to a simmer, then cook for 7 minutes. Remove from heat, cover and set aside for 20 minutes or until water is completely absorbed. Transfer to a large bowl with the soy beans.

Meanwhile, heat 1 tbs olive oil in a saucepan over medium heat. Add leek and celery, and cook for 2-3 minutes until leek softens. Remove from pan and set aside.

Heat remaining 1 tbs olive oil in the same saucepan over high heat and cook mushrooms for 2-3 minutes until softened. Season well with sea salt and freshly ground black pepper. Cool slightly, then transfer to the rice mixture with the leek mixture, linseeds, half the spring onion and 1 tbs toasted sesame seeds, then stir to combine.

Whisk together soy sauce, lemon juice, sugar and remaining 1 tsp sesame oil and 1 tsp sesame seeds in a small bowl, then toss through the salad. Divide among 4 bowls and serve topped with remaining spring onion. **Serves 4**

WARM SPICED QUINOA & CHICKEN SALAD

2 tbs olive oil

6 skinless chicken thigh
  fillets, cut into 2cm pieces

1 onion, finely chopped

2 garlic cloves,
  finely chopped

1 tbs grated ginger

1 long green chilli, seeds
  removed, finely chopped

1 tbs panch phoran

2 tsp mild curry powder

400g quinoa

500ml chicken stock

120g frozen peas, blanched,
  drained

45g coriander,
finely chopped

Micro herbs (such as
  amaranth, optional),
  to garnish

Thick Greek-style yoghurt
  and pappadums, to serve

Heat 1 tbs oil in a large frypan over high heat. Brown half the chicken for 2 minutes each side or until golden, then set aside. Repeat with remaining 1 tbs oil and chicken.

Reduce heat to medium-high, add onion to same pan and cook, stirring, for 3-4 minutes until softened. Add garlic, ginger, chilli, panch phoran and curry powder, stir for 1 minute or until fragrant, then add quinoa and stock. Return chicken and any cooking juices to the pan, bring to a simmer, then reduce heat to low and cook for 20 minutes or until chicken is cooked and liquid absorbed. Stir through peas and coriander, scatter over micro herbs, if using, and serve warm or at room temperature with yoghurt and pappadums.

Serves 4-6

THAI SMOKED CHICKEN SALAD

½ Chinese cabbage,
   shredded
2 baby cos lettuce,
   shredded
½ red onion, thinly sliced
3 smoked chicken breast
   fillets, shredded
100g roasted unsalted
   peanuts
1 bunch coriander,
   leaves picked
2 carrots
1 cucumber
2 tbs fish sauce
2 tbs sweet chilli sauce
2 tbs rice vinegar
2 tsp grated ginger
Juice of 1 lime

Place cabbage, lettuce, onion, chicken, half the peanuts and half the coriander leaves in a bowl.

Using a vegetable peeler, shave carrots and cucumber into long ribbons and add to the bowl.

Whisk fish and sweet chilli sauces, rice vinegar, grated ginger and lime juice in a small bowl. Add dressing to the bowl and toss well to combine.

Serve salad topped with remaining peanuts and coriander.

Serves 4-6

PUMPKIN CAPRESE SALAD

1/2 small Japanese pumpkin (kabocha), sliced into thin wedges
165ml olive oil
1/2 tsp chilli flakes
75g plain flour, seasoned
2 scamorza, sliced
250g cherry tomatoes, halved
2 tbs balsamic vinegar
1/2 bunch basil, leaves picked

Preheat oven to 180°C (gas mark 4). Line a large baking tray with baking paper.

Place pumpkin on the tray and drizzle over 2 tbs olive oil. Scatter with chilli flakes, season with sea salt and freshly ground black pepper, then roast for 25-30 minutes until tender.

Place seasoned flour in a shallow bowl. Lightly dust the scamorza slices with flour, shaking off excess. Heat another 2 tbs oil in a large frypan over medium-high heat and cook half the slices for 1 minute each side or until golden. Transfer to the oven to keep warm. Repeat with another 2 tbs oil and remaining cheese slices.

Place pumpkin and cheese slices on a board or platter. Add tomatoes, drizzle with balsamic vinegar and remaining 2 tbs oil, and season well. Scatter over basil just before serving. **Serves 6-8**

LABNE

Combine 500g thick, Greek-style yoghurt and 2 tsp salt, then place in the centre of a clean piece of muslin or J cloth and tie the ends to form a bundle.

Place in a sieve set over a bowl in the fridge and leave for at least 5 hours or overnight to drain.

Roll into golf-ball-size balls and place in a sterilised jar with some woody herbs, such as rosemary, thyme and oregano, and a garlic clove.

Pour in enough olive oil to cover. Store in the fridge for up to 1 week.

VINAIGRETTE

Whisk together 1 tsp Dijon mustard, 1 tsp very finely chopped garlic and 60ml Champagne or white wine vinegar in a small bowl.

Slowly whisk in 125ml extra virgin olive oil until emulsified.

Season with sea salt and freshly ground black pepper.

GREEK SALAD WITH CALAMARI

2 mini cos lettuces,
  leaves separated
250g cherry tomatoes,
  halved
1 telegraph cucumber,
  cut into 2cm pieces
75g pitted kalamata olives
340g polenta
2 tbs finely chopped
  flat-leaf parsley
250ml buttermilk
500g squid tubes, cleaned,
  sliced into rings
750ml peanut (groundnut)
  oil, to deep-fry
1/2 quantity of vinaigrette
  (see Essentials, p 189)
125g feta, crumbled

Place lettuce, tomato, cucumber and olives in a bowl.

Combine polenta and parsley in a bowl. Place buttermilk in a bowl and season with sea salt and freshly ground black pepper. Dip calamari first into buttermilk, allowing excess to drain back into bowl, then coat in polenta mixture, gently shaking off excess.

Heat oil in a deep-fryer or large saucepan to 180°C (gas mark 4) (a cube of bread will turn golden in 35 seconds when the oil is hot enough) and cook calamari, in batches, until crisp and golden.

Toss salad with vinaigrette dressing, scatter over feta and serve with calamari. **Serves 4**

FATTOUSH WITH LABNE

1 tsp cumin seeds

60ml extra virgin olive oil

1 tbs finely chopped
    preserved lemon rind
    (see Essentials, p 116)

2 tbs lemon juice

1½ tbs red wine vinegar

1 tbs finely chopped
    flat-leaf parsley

1 garlic clove,
    finely chopped

1 Lebanese flatbread,
    baked until crisp, cooled,
    broken into shards

1 baby cos lettuce,
    inner leaves only, torn

50g each baby spinach,
    wild rocket and lamb's
    lettuce

175g mixed olives

1 cucumber, peeled, finely
    chopped

2 roma (plum) tomatoes,
    seeds removed, finely
    chopped

1 tbs sumac, plus extra
    to dust

4 balls of labne (see
    Essentials, p 188)

Labne is so easy to make, and a staple well worth its place in your fridge. Add it to Middle Eastern-style salads, such as this fattoush, tear and scatter it over a spiced couscous, or serve it as part of a mezze with olives, dips and flatbreads.

To make dressing, toast cumin seeds in a small frypan over medium heat, stirring, for 30 seconds or until fragrant. Cool slightly, then transfer to a food processor with oil, preserved lemon, lemon juice, vinegar, parsley and garlic, then pulse until smooth.

Combine remaining ingredients, except for labne, in a large bowl and drizzle with the dressing. Tear labne over the top and serve dusted with extra sumac. **Serves 4**

BLACK RICE, PRAWN & MANGO SALAD

200g black rice
300g cooked peeled
    prawns (tails intact)
1 mango, cheeks halved,
    thinly sliced
4 spring onions, thinly sliced
1 tbs finely chopped
    coriander, plus extra
    leaves to serve
1 long red chilli, seeds
    removed, finely chopped
2 tbs rice vinegar
2 tbs light soy sauce
Juice of 1 lime
1 tsp grated ginger
1 tsp sesame oil
60ml vegetable oil
75g chopped roasted
    unsalted peanuts

Whether you believe in the concept of 'super foods' or not, black rice has good credentials. This dark purple whole grain is not just beautiful; its colour is produced by anthocyanin, also found in blueberries, so it's good for you, too. Legend has it that in China, it was known as 'forbidden rice' because it was reserved for the nobility due to its health-giving powers. These days, it's sold in supermarkets – far more democratic!

Cook rice according to packet instructions, rinse under cold running water, drain, then set aside to cool.

Transfer cooled rice to a bowl with prawns, mango, spring onion and coriander, then toss to combine.

Whisk chilli, rice vinegar, soy sauce, lime juice, ginger and oils in a small bowl and season with sea salt and freshly ground black pepper. Add to salad, toss gently to combine, then serve scattered with peanuts and extra coriander. **Serves 4**

CONFIT DUCK & LENTIL SALAD

200g dried whole green
   Puy-style lentils
4 confit duck legs
2 tbs pomegranate
   molasses
1/2 quantity of vinaigrette
   (see Essentials, p 261)
1 chicory, shredded
60g watercress,
   leaves picked
2 cooked baby beetroots,
   thickly sliced
4 kumquats in syrup,
   drained, sliced or
   1 orange, segmented
Seeds of 1 pomegranate

Preheat the oven to 180°C (gas mark 4).

Place lentils in a saucepan with enough cold water to cover. Bring to the boil over medium-high heat, then reduce heat to low and simmer, covered, for 20-25 minutes until tender. Drain, then set aside to cool completely.

Scrape excess duck fat from the confit (reserve the fat for frying or roasting potatoes, if desired; see Essentials, p 117). Place duck in a shallow roasting pan and cook for 10 minutes or until crisp. Set aside to cool slightly.

Whisk pomegranate molasses and vinaigrette in a small bowl.

Shred duck meat, discarding skin and bones, and combine with lentils, chicory, watercress, beetroot, kumquat and pomegranate seeds in a bowl. Add dressing, toss to combine and serve. **Serves 4**

CAJUN-INSPIRED CAESAR SALAD

250g cherry tomatoes, halved

2 tbs extra virgin olive oil

1 tsp coriander seeds

1/2 tsp yellow mustard seeds

1 tsp cumin seeds

2 tsp paprika

1 tsp garlic powder

2 tbs onion powder

1/2 tsp cayenne pepper

1 tsp dried oregano

1 tsp dried thyme

6 bacon rashers

120g creme fraiche or sour cream

2 tbs mayonnaise (see Essentials, p 68) or store-bought whole-egg mayonnaise

2 tbs red wine vinegar

4 soft-boiled eggs (see Essentials, p 21), peeled

2 small baby cos lettuces

12 slices baguette, toasted

Preheat the oven to 120°C (gas mark 1/2).

Place tomatoes on a baking tray, drizzle with oil and season with sea salt and freshly ground black pepper. Roast for 1 1/2 hours or until tomatoes start to collapse. Set aside.

To make Cajun spice mix, place coriander, mustard and cumin seeds, paprika, garlic and onion powders, cayenne, oregano and thyme in a frypan and stir over medium heat for 30 seconds or until fragrant. Transfer to a spice grinder or mortar and pestle, and grind to a fine powder. Place in a small, shallow bowl.

Cook bacon in a frypan over medium-high heat for 2 minutes each side or until crisp and golden. Drain on paper towel, then break into shards.

Combine creme fraiche, mayonnaise, vinegar and 1 tsp Cajun spice mix in a small bowl. Season with sea salt.

Pat eggs dry, roll in some Cajun spice mix, then cut in half.

Cut lettuces lengthways into wedges and arrange on a platter with eggs, bacon, tomatoes and toasted baguette. Drizzle over a little of the Cajun dressing and sprinkle over a little extra Cajun spice to serve. **Serves 4**

ICING → sugar

DESSERTS

Mmmm...

Toasted grated
coconut

Lemon
curd

Dutch
cocoa

CASTER
sugar

BROWN
sugar

SUMMER PUDDING FRENCH TOAST

200g frozen mixed berries
100g caster sugar
250g strawberries, hulled,
 halved if large
1 vanilla bean, split,
 seeds scraped
200ml single cream
1 egg, lightly beaten
4 thick slices brioche
30g unsalted butter
Thick cream or Greek-style
 yoghurt, to serve

Place berries in a saucepan over low heat with 75g sugar and 2 tbs water, stirring until sugar dissolves. Simmer for 3-4 minutes, then set aside to cool slightly. Puree in a blender or press through a sieve into a bowl, discarding solids. Add strawberries and vanilla pod and seeds, then cover and refrigerate for at least 2 hours or overnight for the flavours to develop.

Whisk cream, egg and remaining 25g sugar until combined. Dip brioche in cream mixture, soaking each slice for about 20 seconds. Heat butter in a frypan over medium heat, then cook brioche for 1-2 minutes each side until golden.

To serve, divide brioche among plates and top with strawberries and syrup, and a dollop of cream or yoghurt. **Serves 4**

STICKY TOFFEE GINGER PUDDING

1 x 500g store-bought
   ginger cake, cut into
   12 slices
Vanilla ice cream, to serve
$^1/_2$ quantity of unsalted
   caramel sauce (see
   Essentials, p 261)
50g stem ginger in syrup,
   chopped

This would have to be one of the easiest desserts to put together. I like to keep a ginger cake in my freezer for when I need to come up with a pudding in a hurry.

Preheat the oven to 170°C (gas mark 3).

Wrap cake slices together in foil and place in the oven for 10 minutes or until warm.

To serve, layer 3 slices of the warmed cake on each of 4 plates with tablespoonfuls of vanilla ice cream, drizzle over caramel sauce and top with chopped stem ginger. **Serves 4**

RUM & RAISIN ICE CREAM

85g raisins
125ml dark rum
395g can sweetened
    condensed milk
600ml double cream
1 tbs instant coffee,
    dissolved in 2 tbs boiling
    water, cooled

Begin this recipe 1 day ahead.

Soak raisins in rum for at least 4 hours or overnight.
    Using electric beaters, whisk together condensed milk and cream
to soft peaks. Gently fold in the raisin and coffee mixtures. Transfer
to an airtight container and freeze overnight. **Makes 1.2 litres**

SURPRISE RASPBERRY SOUFFLES

25g unsalted butter,
  melted, cooled, to brush
75g caster sugar, plus extra
  to dust
3 x 125g punnets
  raspberries
5 egg whites
6 undusted chocolate
  truffles (see Essentials,
  p 213)
Icing sugar and shaved
  chocolate curls, to serve

The 'surprise' in these soufflés is a molten chocolate truffle in the centre. Serve the remaining chocolate truffles as petits fours with coffee, or store them in the fridge for another occasion – although I doubt they'll last that long.

Preheat the oven to 200°C (gas mark 6). Working in upward brushstrokes from the bottom to the top of each ramekin, brush 6 x 200ml ramekins with melted butter, then liberally dust with extra caster sugar, gently tapping ramekins to remove excess sugar.

Process raspberries in a food processor, then press through a sieve, discarding solids, to give 250ml puree. Add 1 tbs caster sugar and stir until sugar dissolves.

Using electric beaters, whisk egg whites to soft peaks. Whisking constantly, slowly add remaining 55g caster sugar and whisk to stiff peaks. Gently fold a quarter of the egg white mixture into puree to loosen, then fold in the remaining egg white mixture. Using a piping bag, if possible, pipe raspberry mixture to half-fill the ramekins. Add a truffle to each one, then pipe raspberry mixture on top to fill to the rim of the ramekin. Smooth top with a palette knife, then run your thumb gently around the inside of the ramekins (this will help the soufflés to rise). Bake for 7 minutes or until well risen and golden on top.

Serve soufflés dusted with icing sugar and topped with chocolate curls. **Serves 6**

TUTTI FRUTTI STEAMED PUDDINGS

185g unsalted butter,
  softened
165g caster sugar
2 eggs
2 tsp finely grated
  lemon zest
225g self-raising flour
125ml milk
1 quantity of custard (see
  Essentials, p 20), or single
  cream, to serve

Toppings
Lemon curd (see Essentials,
  p 237)
Strawberry jam
Blackcurrant jam
Orange marmalade
Ginger marmalade with
  chopped stem ginger
Orange conserve
Fig jam with sliced fresh figs

The idea behind these puddings is to serve them with different toppings. The ones we've listed here are just suggestions – the only limit is your imagination!

Preheat the oven to 170°C (gas mark 3).

Grease and line the bases and sides of 6 x 250ml dariole moulds. Place ½ tablespoons of your preferred topping in each.

Using electric beaters, beat butter and sugar until thick and pale. Add eggs 1 at a time, beating well after each addition. Fold in lemon zest. Sift over flour and fold in until combined, then stir through the milk until mixture is a soft dropping consistency.

Divide batter among moulds, filling to 1cm from rim to allow for rising. Cover each mould first with a piece of pleated baking paper, then a piece of pleated foil and secure with kitchen string.

Place moulds in a roasting pan and pour in enough boiling water to come halfway up sides. Bake for 40-45 minutes until a skewer inserted into the centre of the puddings comes out clean. Remove ramekins from pan and set aside puddings to rest for 5 minutes.

Turn out puddings onto a platter and top each with another ½ tablespoon of topping. Serve with custard or cream. **Serves 6**

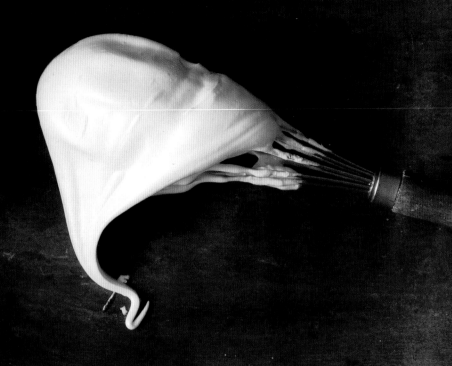

CLASSIC MERINGUES

Preheat the oven to 120°C (gas mark ½).

Place 220g caster sugar and
4 room-temperature egg whites in a bowl
set over a pan of gently simmering water.

Whisk with a balloon whisk until sugar
completely dissolves.

Transfer to the bowl of an electric mixer
and whisk for 3 minutes or until very thick
and glossy, then add ½ tsp vanilla extract.

Drop tablespoonfuls of meringue
onto 2 lined baking trays and transfer
to the oven.

Reduce oven to 90°C (gas mark ¼) and
bake for 1½ hours or until dry and crisp.

Store meringues for up to 1 week in an
airtight container. **Makes 12**

EASY CHOCOLATE TRUFFLES

Place 125ml double cream and 90g chopped unsalted butter in a microwave-safe bowl and microwave for 1 minute or until butter melts and cream is hot but not boiling.

Add 300g finely chopped dark chocolate and stand for 2-3 minutes until melted.

Stir until smooth, then add 2 tbs brandy or whisky.

Refrigerate until mixture is firm.

Toss heaped teaspoons of the mixture in cocoa powder, coconut or finely chopped nuts to coat.

Chill for at least 1 hour before serving.
Makes 25

CHOCOLATE HAZELNUT CHEESECAKE

300g plain chocolate
 biscuits
80g unsalted butter,
 melted, cooled
250g cream cheese,
 at room temperature
220g chocolate hazelnut
 spread (we used Nutella)
1 tsp vanilla extract
2 tbs amaretto
500ml double cream
Shaved chocolate and
 chopped toasted
 hazelnuts, to serve

Sharing plates are all the rage, so serving this simple 'cheesecake' in a jar for everyone to help themselves will certainly give your guests something to talk about.

Using a food processor, pulse biscuits to form crumbs. Add to butter and stir to combine well, then press crumb mixture into the base of a 2L glass jar or bowl.

Whiz cream cheese, chocolate hazelnut spread, vanilla and amaretto in a clean food processor until smooth. Transfer to a bowl.

Whisk 300ml cream to soft peaks, then fold into the cream cheese mixture until well combined. Spoon over the biscuit base, then refrigerate for 4 hours.

To serve, whisk remaining 200ml cream to soft peaks and spoon over the cream cheese mixture, then decorate with shaved chocolate and toasted hazelnuts. **Serves 8**

CRUMBLY OLIVE OIL, ROSEMARY & PEAR CAKE

225g plain flour

120g wholemeal
   or spelt flour

165g caster sugar

1½ tsp baking powder

3 eggs

310ml fruity extra virgin
   olive oil

1 tsp vanilla extract

4 small pears, peeled,
   cored, cut into 1cm
   pieces

2 tsp chopped rosemary
   leaves

35g currants

Mascarpone, to serve

There are times when you tire of rich desserts, which is when a simple cake like this comes into its own. I first tasted a similar one in Italy and loved it. Try to use a fruity olive oil and soak the currants overnight in Marsala or brandy if you like, to add an authentic Italian flavour.

Preheat the oven to 180°C (gas mark 4). Grease a 26cm, 3cm-deep loose-bottom tart pan.

Sift together flours into a bowl. Add sugar and baking powder. Beat eggs, olive oil and vanilla, then add to flour mixture, stirring to combine. Gently fold through pear, rosemary and currants (with any soaking liquor, if using). Spoon batter into tart pan, then bake for 55 minutes or until cake is golden and a skewer comes out clean when inserted into the cake. Cool in pan for 10 minutes, then transfer to a wire rack to cool completely. Serve warm or at room temperature with mascarpone. **Serves 6-8**

SALTED CHOCOLATE CARAMEL POTS

200g caster sugar
500ml double cream
3 egg yolks
1 tsp vanilla extract
1 tbs sea salt
300g good-quality milk
    chocolate, chopped
Whipped cream (optional),
    to serve

Salted caramel
220g caster sugar
2 tsp sea salt flakes

To make caramel cream, combine sugar and 2 tbs water in a saucepan over low heat, stirring until sugar dissolves. Increase heat to medium-high and cook, without stirring, occasionally brushing down sides of pan with a little cold water to remove sugar crystals, for 6-8 minutes until a golden caramel forms. Remove from the heat and slowly add 200ml cream (be careful, as mixture will bubble). Return to the heat and stir until smooth. Cool slightly, then add 1 egg yolk and stir to combine. Divide among 6 x 200ml pots or glasses, cover and refrigerate for 2 hours or until set.

Meanwhile, to make salted chocolate cream, place remaining 300ml cream in a saucepan over medium heat, add vanilla and salt, stirring until salt dissolves, then bring to the boil. Remove from heat, then add chocolate and stand for 2-3 minutes until chocolate melts. Stir until smooth and combined, then cool slightly. Add remaining 2 egg yolks and stir to combine, then pour over the chilled caramel cream. Refrigerate for 2-3 hours or overnight to set.

To make salted caramel, line a baking tray with foil and brush with a flavourless oil, such as vegetable. Combine sugar in a saucepan with 60ml cold water over low heat, stirring until sugar dissolves. Increase heat to medium and cook, without stirring, occasionally brushing down sides of pan with a little cold water to remove sugar crystals, for 6-8 minutes until a deep golden caramel forms. Immediately pour caramel into tray, then sprinkle over sea salt flakes. Cool completely, then break into shards.

Serve pots topped with salted caramel shards and whipped cream, if desired. **Serves 6**

RHUBARB ETON MESS

1 large bunch (to give 500g)
   rhubarb, trimmed, cut
   into 3cm lengths
75g caster sugar
1 egg
1 tsp vanilla extract
250g mascarpone
125ml double cream
3 meringues (see Essentials,
   p 212), to serve

Place rhubarb in a saucepan with 55g sugar and 60ml water, then cook over a low heat for 5-6 minutes until tender but still holding its shape.

Using a wooden spoon, beat egg and remaining 20g sugar with vanilla. Add mascarpone and 2 tbs cream, and beat to combine.

Using a balloon whisk, whisk remaining 80ml cream to soft peaks, then gently fold through the mascarpone mixture.

Dollop a dessertspoonful mascarpone mixture in the centre of each of 6 plates, then, using a slotted spoon, arrange some rhubarb around each. Crumble meringue around, then drizzle with rhubarb poaching liquid. Alternatively, layer rhubarb, mascarpone and crumbled meringue in 6 x 200ml glasses. **Serves 6**

LEMON TIRAMISU

Juice of 1 lemon
75g caster sugar
250g mascarpone
100ml limoncello
250g good-quality
   store-bought sponge cake,
   cut into 2.5cm pieces
325g lemon curd (see
   Essentials, p 237)

Candied lemon zest
220g caster sugar
Finely shredded zest
   of 2 lemons

Line a baking tray with baking paper and set a wire rack on top.

To make candied lemon zest, combine sugar and 60ml cold water in a saucepan over low heat, stirring until sugar dissolves. Add lemon zest, increase heat to medium-low and simmer for 5 minutes or until zest is transluscent. Spread zest on the wire rack and set aside.

Meanwhile, to make lemon syrup, combine lemon juice, sugar and 2 tbs water in a saucepan over low heat, stirring until sugar dissolves. Increase heat to medium-low and simmer for 1-2 minutes until slightly reduced. Cool.

Using a balloon whisk, whisk mascarpone and limoncello until well combined.

Divide half the cake among 4 x 200ml dessert glasses, drizzle with half the syrup and top with half the lemon curd, then finally a dollop of mascarpone mixture. Repeat with remaining cake, syrup, lemon curd and mascarpone mixture. Alternatively, layer in a 1L glass bowl. Refrigerate for 30 minutes to set.

Decorate with candied lemon zest to serve. **Serves 4**

REMEMBER
Keep things cool
for pastry but
room temperature
for cakes

Pistachio
Kernels

CAKES & BAKES

Walnut Kernels

SALTED MACADAMIA & CARAMEL TARTS

1 egg white, lightly whisked
100g salted macadamias,
    lightly toasted
300g jar dulce de leche
Icing sugar, to dust
Melted chocolate,
    to drizzle

Sweet shortcrust pastry
225g plain flour
125g chilled unsalted
    butter, chopped
50g icing sugar
1 tsp vanilla extract
1 egg yolk

To make sweet shortcrust pastry, process flour, butter and icing sugar in a food processor to fine breadcrumbs. Add vanilla, egg yolk and 1 tbs iced water, then process until the mixture just comes together. Form into a ball, then enclose in clingfilm and refrigerate for 30 minutes.

Grease 6 x 10cm loose-bottomed tart pans. Roll out pastry on a lightly floured surface to 5mm thick and used to line tart pans. Refrigerate for 15 minutes.

Preheat the oven to 190°C (gas mark 5). Prick pastry bases with a fork, then line with baking paper and fill with rice or pastry weights. Bake for 10 minutes, then remove paper and weights.

Brush the insides of the pastry bases with egg white, then return to the oven for a further 2-3 minutes until golden, dry and crisp. Set aside to cool.

Fill the cooled tart bases with dulce de leche, then divide macadamias among the tarts. Dust with icing sugar and drizzle with melted chocolate to serve. **Serves 6**

LAZY LEMON TART

1 quantity sweet shortcrust
  pastry (see recipe p 226)
  or store-bought
  shortcrust or sweet
  shortcrust pastry
1 large lemon, seeds
  removed, chopped
330g caster sugar
110g softened unsalted
  butter
1 tsp vanilla extract
4 eggs
60ml double cream
Icing sugar and thick cream,
  to serve

This an amazing tart, as you just throw the filling
ingredients in a blender. But note that it won't work
in a food processor; you need a blender with a strong
motor in order to chop the whole lemon, skin and all.

Grease a 23cm loose-bottomed tart pan. Roll out pastry on
a lightly floured surface to 5mm thick and use to line tart pan.
Refrigerate for 30 minutes.

Preheat the oven to 190°C (gas mark 5). Line tart case with baking
paper and fill with rice or pastry weights. Bake for 8 minutes,
remove paper and weights, then bake for a further 3 minutes or
until dry and crisp.

Meanwhile, place lemon, sugar, butter, vanilla and eggs in
a high-speed blender. Blend until smooth, add double cream and
pulse quickly to just combine. Pour lemon mixture into tart shell,
then bake for 30 minutes or until just set. Cool tart in pan, then
dust with icing sugar and serve at room temperature with thick
cream. **Serves 6-8**

RED WINE CHOCOLATE CAKE

200g plain flour

2 tbs cocoa powder,
    plus extra to dust

1 tsp baking powder

1/2 tsp bicarbonate of soda

225g softened unsalted
    butter

220g caster sugar

4 eggs

200g dark chocolate,
    melted, cooled

1 tsp vanilla extract

125ml milk

125ml red wine

Raspberries in raspberry
    syrup (see Essentials,
    p 236), and whipped
    cream, to serve

Ganache

150g dark chocolate,
    chopped

125ml single cream

20g unsalted butter

Ever wondered what to do with those last few drops of red wine left in the bottle? Use it in a simple chocolate cake for added depth of flavour.

Preheat the oven to 160°C (gas mark 3). Grease a 2.4L bundt pan.

Sift together flour, cocoa, baking powder and bicarbonate of soda onto a sheet of baking paper.

Using an electric mixer, beat the butter and sugar for 3-4 minutes until thick and pale. Add eggs 1 at a time, beating well after each addition. Gently fold in melted chocolate until combined. Beating gently, slowly add flour mixture until combined, then add vanilla, milk and red wine, and beat to combine. Spoon batter into prepared pan, levelling the top with the back of the spoon.

Bake for 45-50 minutes until a skewer comes out clean when inserted into the cake. Cool cake in pan for 10 minutes before turning out onto a wire rack to cool completely.

Meanwhile, to make ganache, place all ingredients in a bowl set over a saucepan of gently simmering water (don't let the bowl touch the water) for 3-4 minutes until chocolate melts. Remove bowl from pan, stir until well combined, then allow to cool at room temperature.

To serve, dust cake with extra cocoa, then drizzle over the ganache and serve with raspberries in raspberry syrup and whipped cream. **Serves 8**

PANETTONE CAKE

250g sultanas

60ml Marsala
   or brandy

600g panettone or brioche
   loaf, thickly sliced

80g softened unsalted
   butter

100g dried cranberries

8 eggs

600ml double cream

250ml milk

150g caster sugar

1 tsp vanilla extract

Icing sugar and single
   cream, to serve

Place sultanas and Marsala in a small bowl and set aside to soak for 30 minutes.

Grease a 24cm springform cake pan. Place a double piece of paper towel on a baking tray and set the pan on top (some egg mixture will seep through the bottom of the cake pan, so the paper will absorb it).

Spread each slice of panettone with butter, then layer slices in the pan, scattering sultana mixture and cranberries over each layer.

Whisk together eggs, cream, milk, caster sugar and vanilla until combined. Pour egg mixture over the layered panettone, then set aside for 30 minutes for the egg mixture to soak in.

Preheat the oven to 150°C (gas mark 2). Remove paper towel from baking tray, then transfer tray with cake pan to the oven and bake for 1¼ hours or until just set. Rest for 15 minutes in the pan before turning out.

Dust with icing sugar and serve with cream. **Serves 6-8**

SWEET SLIDERS

450g plain flour
1¹/₂ tbs caster sugar
3 tsp dried instant yeast
1 egg, lightly beaten
60g softened unsalted
  butter
250ml milk, heated, plus
  extra to brush
200ml double cream
1 tbs sifted icing sugar,
  plus extra to dust
Scraped seeds of 1 vanilla
  bean or 1 tsp vanilla
  extract
160g strawberry jam
Sliced strawberries,
  to serve

Savoury sliders are menu staples these days – soft little brioche buns with all manner of fillings, from pulled pork and tender Japanese wagyu beef to chargrilled prawns. They're the perfect bite-size morsel, so I thought, why not make them sweet for a change.

Combine flour, caster sugar and yeast in a bowl. Add ¹/₂ tsp salt and make a well in the centre. Add egg, butter and 250ml warm milk, then stir with a wooden spoon to make a soft dough, adding more milk if necessary. Place in an oiled bowl, cover with a clean tea towel and set aside to prove in a warm place for 1 hour or until doubled in size.

Preheat the oven to 190°C (gas mark 5). Grease a 26cm round cake pan. Turn out dough onto a lightly floured surface and knead for 3 minutes or until smooth and elastic. Divide into 12 portions, then shape each into a ball and place side by side in the pan. Cover with a clean tea towel and set aside to prove in a warm place for a further 20 minutes.

Brush tops with extra milk, then bake for 20-25 minutes or until golden. Remove from pan and transfer to a wire rack to cool.

Meanwhile, whisk cream, icing sugar and vanilla seeds to soft peaks.

To serve, split each bun in half, spread with strawberry jam, top with cream and sliced strawberries, sandwich halves together and dust with icing sugar. **Makes 12**

RASPBERRY SAUCE

Puree 250g raspberries, 2 tbs kirsch and 2 tbs caster sugar in a blender, then press through a sieve and discard solids.

LEMON CURD

Using a balloon whisk, beat 220g caster sugar, 175ml lemon juice, 3 eggs, 3 egg yolks and 1 tsp vanilla extract in a bowl.

Set the bowl over a saucepan of gently simmering water and whisk constantly until the mixture is thick. Remove from the heat, then whisk in 70g chopped softened unsalted butter and a pinch of sea salt until combined.

Strain through a sieve, then transfer to sterilised jars and cool before sealing. Store for up to 1 month in the fridge. **Makes 600ml.**

MONKEY BUN

310g unsalted butter
500g plain flour
1¼ tbs dried instant yeast
1 tbs caster sugar
1 tbs finely grated
  orange zest
1 tsp ground cinnamon
180ml warm milk
2 eggs, lightly beaten
200g brown sugar
1 tbs golden syrup
12 pitted cherries, or other
  seasonal berries or small
  pieces of chocolate

This recipe is inspired by the wonderful Sally Wise, whose eponymous cooking school in Tasmania is a mecca for anyone wanting to learn the art of preserving and slow-cooking. Sally serves this to her students on arrival and it certainly sets the scene for a day of fine cooking.

Melt 60g butter in a small saucepan over low heat, then cool.

Combine flour, yeast, caster sugar, zest, cinnamon and 1 tsp sea salt in a bowl. Make a well in the centre, then add melted butter, milk and eggs, and stir well to combine. Place in an oiled bowl, cover with a clean tea towel and set aside to prove in a warm place for 1½ hours or until doubled in size.

Place remaining 250g butter, sugar and golden syrup in a pan over low heat, stirring until melted and combined.

Grease a 2.5L kugelhopf pan. Knock down dough, turn out onto a lightly floured surface and knead for 3-4 minutes until smooth and elastic. Divide dough into 12 portions and form into balls. Push a cherry into the centre of each, pinching dough to encase the fruit completely. Dip each dough ball into syrup, turning until well coated, then layer in the prepared pan, pouring over any remaining syrup. Cover with a clean tea towel and set aside to prove in a warm place for a further 1 hour or until the dough has risen to reach the top of the mould.

Preheat the oven to 190°C (gas mark 5). Place pan on a baking tray (some sauce may bubble over during baking). Bake for 10 minutes, then reduce to 160°C (gas mark 3) and bake for a further 20-25 minutes. Stand in the pan for 5 minutes before carefully turning out onto a plate to serve. **Serves 6-8**

GREEK APPLE PIE

110g caster sugar

1 cinnamon quill

1 vanilla bean, split

80g sultanas

2 Granny Smith apples,
  peeled, cored,
  cut into 2cm pieces
  (to give 500g) chopped
  apple)

2 tbs maple syrup,
  plus extra to drizzle

60g finely chopped walnuts

1 tsp ground cinnamon

60g brown sugar

8 sheets filo pastry

80g unsalted butter,
  melted, cooled

2 tbs chopped pistachio
  nuts

Icing sugar, to dust

Preheat the oven to 180°C (gas mark 4). Grease a 24cm springform cake pan.

Place caster sugar, cinnamon quill, vanilla and sultanas in a saucepan with 250ml water. Bring to a simmer over medium-low heat, stirring until sugar dissolves, then cook for 10 minutes or until reduced. Add apple and cook for a further 6-8 minutes until tender. Add maple syrup, stir to combine, then set aside to cool.

Combine walnuts, ground cinnamon and brown sugar in a bowl.

Working with 1 sheet of filo at a time and keeping the others covered with a lightly dampened tea towel to prevent them from drying out, lightly brush filo sheet with melted butter. Sprinkle with a quarter of the nut mixture, top with another filo sheet, brush with butter and spread a quarter of the apple mixture along the long edge. Roll up from the long edge and brush with butter, then repeat with remaining mixture and filo until you have 4 rolls. Coil rolls in pan to form a spiral (if rolls crack, patch with extra filo brushed with butter).

Bake for 25 minutes or until golden. To serve, drizzle with extra maple syrup, scatter over pistachios and dust with icing sugar.

Serves 6

PEANUT BUTTER CHEESECAKE

400g digestive biscuits

50g ground almonds

120g unsalted butter,
  melted, cooled

350g fresh ricotta, drained

500g cream cheese

250g brown sugar

4 eggs

280g peanut butter
  (crunchy or smooth)

1 tsp vanilla extract

300ml single cream

300ml sour cream

200ml double cream

12 peanut butter chocolates
  (optional)

Grease a 23cm springform cake pan.

Combine biscuits and ground almonds in a food processor and pulse to the consistency of coarse breadcrumbs. Add butter and pulse until mixture just comes together. Press mixture into the base of the cake pan, then refrigerate for 30 minutes.

Preheat the oven to 160°C (gas mark 3).

Place ricotta, cream cheese and brown sugar in the bowl of an electric mixer and beat for 1-2 minutes until smooth. Add eggs 1 at a time, beating well after each addition. Add peanut butter, vanilla, single cream and sour cream, then beat on low speed until mixture is smooth and combined.

Spread ricotta mixture over the biscuit base, then wrap the outside base and side of the cake pan with a double sheet of aluminium foil, ensuring there are no gaps. Place pan in a deep baking pan, then pour in enough water to come halfway up the side. Bake for 1 1/2 hours or until cheesecake is almost set, but the centre still has a slight wobble. Turn off the oven and set the oven door ajar with a wooden spoon. Leave cheesecake to cool in the oven for 1 hour, then remove and refrigerate for 3 hours.

Whisk double cream to soft peaks, then spread over the top of the cheesecake. Break chocolates into chunks, if using, and scatter over the top. Serve with a health warning! **Serves 8-10**

SCANDI CAKE

250g softened unsalted
   butter
220g caster sugar
3 eggs
225g self-raising flour
100g plain flour
60ml milk
1½ tbs lemon juice
Assorted toppings, to serve
   (we used dulce de leche,
   lemon curd (see
   Essentials, p 237),
   raspberry sauce (see
   Essentials, p 236), fresh
   fruit, chopped nuts and
   thick cream)

The idea of this cake is to slice and serve it like a sweet smorgasbord. Arrange all your favourite toppings in small dishes along with a variety of fruits and nuts, then let your guests pick and choose.

Preheat the oven to 170°C (gas mark 3). Grease a 10cm x 21cm loaf pan and line base and sides with baking paper.

Beat butter and sugar with electric beaters for 3-4 minutes until thick and pale. Add eggs 1 at a time, beating well after each addition. Sift in flours, then stir through milk and lemon juice.

Spoon batter into the pan, then bake for 1 hour (cover loosely with foil if browning too quickly) or until a skewer inserted into the centre comes out clean.

Cool cake in the pan for 10 minutes, then transfer to a wire rack to cool completely. To serve, thickly slice cake and serve with your choice of toppings, fruit, nuts and thick cream. **Serves 6-8**

BLUEBERRY & LEMON SCONES WITH LEMON DRIZZLE ICING

300ml single cream

300g plain flour

1 tsp baking powder

2 tbs caster sugar

100g unsalted butter,
  cut into small pieces

2 tsp finely grated lemon
  zest, plus ½-1 tbs juice

125g punnet blueberries

150g sifted icing sugar

Whipped cream and lemon
  curd (see Essentials,
  p 237), to serve

Preheat the oven to 220°C (gas mark 7). Grease and flour a baking tray.

Set aside 1tbs single cream to brush tops of scones.

Sift flour and baking powder into a bowl. Add sugar and ½ tsp salt, then rub the butter into the flour mixture until the consistency of fine breadcrumbs. Add lemon zest, blueberries and remaining single cream, and, using a fork, stir until the mixture comes together in a soft, slightly sticky dough. Turn out onto a lightly floured surface and, using your hands, bring the dough together into a ball. Gently press out into a 20cm round, then cut into 8 wedges and place, slightly apart, on baking tray. Brush tops with reserved 1 tbs cream, then bake for 10-12 minutes until golden.

Meanwhile, place icing sugar in a bowl and gradually add enough lemon juice to make a soft drizzle icing.

Cool the scones on a wire rack, then drizzle with icing and serve with whipped cream and lemon curd. **Makes 8**

Blood
plum

Look for ruby red
strawberries for
best flavour.

Raspberries →

Fig ↗

Pomegranate ↓

FRUIT

Blueberries ↙

GIANT PAVLOVA WITH BERRIES & SALTED CARAMEL

6 egg whites

350g caster sugar

1 tbs white balsamic vinegar

1 tbs cornflour, sifted

50g icing sugar, sifted

600ml double cream

500g mixed berries

1 quantity of salted
caramel sauce
(see Essentials, p 261)

The friend who introduced me to this recipe calls it "divine chaos", and you can see why from the picture opposite. The idea is to put the pavlova in the centre of the table, give everyone a spoon and let them go for it!

Preheat oven to 150°C (gas mark 2). Line a large baking tray with baking paper.

Place egg whites in the clean, dry bowl of an electric mixer and whisk for 3-4 minutes on high speed to soft peaks. Add caster sugar, 1 tablespoon at a time, allowing each to be incorporated before adding the next, whisking until mixture is glossy. Reduce speed to low, then add balsamic, cornflour and icing sugar, beating to combine. Spread mixture over the baking paper in a round or oblong shape, making a slight indent in the centre. Reduce oven to 130°C (gas mark ½) and bake meringue for 1 hour. Turn off oven and leave meringue in the oven for 1-2 hours until cooled completely. Remove from oven and place on a platter or serving board.

To serve, whisk cream to soft peaks, then spread over the centre of the meringue base. Scatter over the berries and drizzle with salted caramel. **Serves 8**

COCONUT JELLY, SUMMER FRUITS AND LEMONGRASS SYRUP

Sunflower oil, to grease
6 titanium-strength
    gelatine leaves
800ml coconut cream
150g caster sugar
1 lemongrass stalk (inner
    core only), bruised
2 kaffir lime leaves
Juice of $1/2$ lime
Assorted seasonal fruits
    (such as mango, guava,
    pineapple, star fruit
    and figs), cut into
    bite-sized pieces
Toasted sesame seeds,
    to serve

Grease a 15cm x 20cm straight-edged pan with oil, then line with clingfilm so that film overhangs the two long sides. Soak gelatine in a bowl of cold water for 5 minutes.

Combine coconut cream and half the sugar in a saucepan over medium heat and bring to a simmer, stirring until sugar dissolves. Squeeze excess water from gelatine and add to saucepan, stirring to combine. Pour into prepared pan, then refrigerate for 4 hours or until set.

Meanwhile, place remaining 75g sugar in a saucepan with 125ml water, stirring until sugar dissolves. Add lemongrass and kaffir lime leaves, and cook, without stirring, for 2 minutes. Remove from heat and set aside for 15 minutes for flavours to develop. Discard lemongrass and kaffir lime leaves, then stir in lime juice. Allow to cool.

Combine the fruit in a large bowl and drizzle over the syrup. Remove the jelly from the fridge, then, using the clingfilm, lift out onto a board. Cut the jelly into cubes roughly the same size as the fruit pieces.

To serve, divide the fruit salad and cubes of coconut jelly among 6 dessert glasses and sprinkle with toasted sesame seeds. **Serves 6**

PLUMS & BLACKBERRIES WITH CRUMBLE AND SPICED CREAM

8 red plums, halved,
　　stones removed
110g caster sugar
1 cinnamon quill
1 vanilla bean, split,
　　seeds scraped
125g blackberries
40g wholemeal flour
35g plain flour
50g chilled unsalted butter,
　　chopped
50g brown sugar
100g walnuts, roughly
　　chopped

Spiced cream
150ml double cream
100g thick Greek-style
　　yoghurt
100g mascarpone
1 tbs caster sugar
$1/2$ tsp vanilla extract
$1/2$ tsp ground cardamom

Preheat the oven to 180°C (gas mark 4).

Place plums, cut-side up, in a baking dish just large enough for them to fit snugly. Scatter with caster sugar, cinnamon and vanilla pod and seeds. Cook for 15 minutes, then scatter over blackberries. Return to oven for a further 15 minutes or until plums are tender and have released their juices. Set aside to cool.

For the crumble, line a baking tray with baking paper. Using a food processor, pulse flours, butter, brown sugar and walnuts to coarse crumbs. Scatter on tray and bake, turning occasionally, for 15-20 minutes until golden. Set aside to cool.

For the spiced cream, combine all ingredients in a bowl and whisk to soft peaks.

To serve, divide plums, berries and roasting juices among 4 bowls and top with crumble and a dollop of spiced cream. **Serves 4**

OATMEAL HOTCAKES WITH BERRY CRUSH

250g plain flour
1¼ tsp baking powder
¼ tsp bicarbonate of soda
60g rolled oats
2 tbs caster sugar
280g thick Greek-style
   yoghurt, plus extra
   to serve
250ml milk
55g unsalted butter,
   melted, plus extra
   to brush
2 eggs
Melted dark chocolate,
   to drizzle (optional)
Icing sugar, to dust

Berry crush
450g fresh or frozen
   blackberries
55g caster sugar
150g blueberries
1 tsp arrowroot
60ml maple syrup

To make berry crush, place blackberries in a saucepan with the sugar and lightly crush with a fork. Simmer over medium-low heat, stirring occasionally, for 2-3 minutes until blackberries start to release their juices. Add blueberries and cook for 2-3 minutes until they start to burst. Combine arrowroot with 2 tbs cold water, stir into berry mixture with maple syrup and cook for 1 minute or until slightly double cream. Set aside to cool.

Sift flour, baking powder, bicarbonate of soda and a pinch of salt into a bowl. Stir in the oats and caster sugar. In a separate bowl, whisk yoghurt, milk, butter and eggs. Gently stir into dry ingredients until just combined. Set aside to rest for 15 minutes.

Heat a non-stick frypan over medium heat, then brush with a little extra melted butter. In batches, add 60ml batter to pan, leaving space for them to spread, and cook until small bubbles appear on the surface. Using a palette knife, flip hotcakes over and cook for a further 2 minutes or until cooked through. Remove from pan, cover and keep warm. Repeat with remaining melted butter and batter.

To serve, stack hotcakes, alternating with berry crush and melted chocolate, if using, then dust with icing sugar. Or serve hotcakes, berry crush and melted chocolate separately for people to help themselves. Serve with extra yoghurt. **Makes 14 hotcakes**

MARSALA-ROASTED PEARS AND GRAPES

50g unsalted butter
125g brown sugar
125ml Marsala
Thickly pared zest
    and juice of 1 orange
1 cinnamon quill
1 vanilla bean, split,
    seeds scraped
4 firm, ripe beurre
    bosc (or conference)
    pears
1/2 lemon
350g seedless red grapes,
    cut into small bunches
Vanilla ice-cream, to serve

Preheat the oven to 180°C (gas mark 4).

Place butter and sugar in a saucepan over low heat, stirring until sugar dissolves. Add Marsala and cook for a further 1 minute. Remove from heat, add orange zest and juice, cinnamon and vanilla pod and seeds, then stir to combine.

Peel and cut pears in half lengthways and remove the cores (leaving stalks intact). Rub pears with the cut side of the lemon to prevent them from browning, then place in a baking tray just large enough for them to fit snugly. Pour over the Marsala mixture, then roast for 45 minutes, basting every 10 minutes. Add grapes and roast for a further 15 minutes or until sauce is reduced and syrupy.

Serve with vanilla ice-cream. **Serves 4**

CREPES

Sift 110g plain flour into a bowl with a pinch of salt.

Whisk 2 eggs with 200ml milk and 80ml water.

Add to the flour gradually, whisking well to combine. Melt 50g butter and add 2 tbs to the batter.

Set aside to rest the batter for 15 minutes.

Brush a 20cm crepe or frypan with a little of the remaining melted butter and heat over a high heat.

Reduce heat to medium-high, add 60ml batter and swirl to coat the base of the pan.

Cook for 1 minute or until golden, then flip with a palette knife and cook for 30 seconds on the other side. (Don't worry if you have to discard the first crepe; it often doesn't work!)

Layer crepes between baking paper and keep warm on a plate over a pan of simmering water. Or freeze for up to 3 months and reheat. **Makes 10 crepes**

SALTED CARAMEL SAUCE

Combine 330g caster sugar with 125ml water in a saucepan over low heat, stirring until sugar dissolves.

Increase heat to medium and cook, without stirring, occasionally brushing down the sides of the pan with a damp pastry brush, for 8-10 minutes until a golden caramel forms.

Remove from heat, then immediately pour in 300ml room-temperature double cream (be careful, as mixture will bubble, then seize).

Return pan to the stove over a low heat, add ½ tsp sea salt and cook sauce, stirring, for 1-2 minutes until smooth. (For plain caramel sauce, leave out the salt at this stage.) Store in an airtight container in the fridge for up to 2 weeks.

RICOTTA BLINTZES WITH BLUEBERRY SAUCE

360g fresh ricotta, drained

105g icing sugar, plus extra
  to dust

Finely grated zest
  of ½ lemon

1 tsp vanilla extract

200g blueberries

2 tbs caster sugar

Juice of 1 lemon

1 cinnamon quill

1 tsp arrowroot

1 quantity cooked crepes
  (see Essentials, p 260)

20g unsalted butter,
  melted, cooled, to brush

Creme fraiche or sour
  cream, to serve

Blintzes, or blini, are an Eastern European classic. They're very similar to French crepes, in that they can be served with savoury or sweet fillings, and are lovely for brunch, afternoon tea or as an indulgent dessert. Try these with your own choice of topping; the raspberry sauce in Essentials, page 236, would also work beautifully with them.

To make ricotta filling, place ricotta, icing sugar, lemon zest and vanilla in a bowl and beat until well combined. Cover with clingfilm and refrigerate for at least 1 hour to chill.

To make blueberry sauce, combine blueberries, caster sugar, lemon juice and cinnamon in a saucepan over medium heat and cook for 2-3 minutes until the berries release their juices. Combine arrowroot with 1 tbs cold water, then add to berry mixture. Cook until slightly thickened. Cool, then refrigerate until needed.

Preheat the oven to 180°C (gas mark 4).

Lay prepared crepes on a workbench, place a heaped tablespoonful of ricotta filling in centre of each crepe, fold in all four sides, then roll up to make parcels. Transfer to a baking tray, seam-side down, brush with melted butter, then bake for 20 minutes or until blintzes are warmed through.

Serve blintzes with blueberry sauce and dollops of creme fraiche. **Serves 4**

CHAMPAGNE STRAWBERRY TRIFLES

450g strawberries, hulled,
  cut into 1cm pieces
50g caster sugar
2 leaves titanium-strength
  gelatine
100ml Champagne or
  sparkling wine
4 savoiardi biscuits, each
  broken into 3 pieces
60ml dessert wine or sherry
1/2 quantity creme patissiere
  (see Essentials, p 20) or
  350ml store-bought
  custard, chilled
150ml double cream
1 tbs icing sugar
Amaretti biscuits,
  to serve

Place 350g strawberries and caster sugar in a heatproof bowl over a saucepan of simmering water and cook gently, stirring occasionally, for 1 hour.

Soak gelatine in a small bowl of cold water for 5 minutes.

Strain berry mixture, discarding solids. Squeeze excess water from gelatine, add to warm strawberry syrup and stir until dissolved. Stir in Champagne, skimming any foam from the top. Cool slightly, then refrigerate for 15-20 minutes until almost set.

Dip savoiardi pieces into the dessert wine, then divide among four 250ml dessert glasses. Divide the remaining 100g berries among glasses, then pour over the strawberry jelly mixture. Refrigerate for 2-3 hours until jelly is set. Spoon over the creme patissiere, then refrigerate for a further 30 minutes or until set.

Meanwhile, whisk cream and icing sugar to soft peaks. Serve trifles topped with cream and crumbled amaretti. **Serves 4**

RASPBERRY, PISTACHIO & ROSE SEMIFREDDO

200g caster sugar

90g honey

5 egg whites

600ml double cream

100g pistachios, roughly
chopped

2 tbs rose syrup
or 2 tsp rosewater,
plus extra to drizzle

2 x 125g punnets
raspberries

Mint sprigs, to serve

You can use the basic semifreddo recipe here as the starting point for all kinds of flavour combinations, but keep in mind that adding alcohol will prevent the mixture from freezing firmly. Begin this recipe 1 day ahead.

Line the base and two long sides of a 1L loaf pan with clingfilm, leaving enough film overhanging both sides to cover pan.

Heat sugar and 125ml water in a saucepan over low heat, stirring until sugar dissolves. Increase heat to medium and simmer for 2-3 minutes until slightly reduced. Add honey and cook for a further 1 minute.

Meanwhile, whisk egg whites in the clean bowl of an electric mixer to soft peaks. Whisking constantly, slowly pour in the hot syrup. Continue whisking until mixture is cold, then transfer to a bowl.

Whisk cream to soft peaks, then gently fold into egg white mixture. Fold in pistachios, rose syrup and half the raspberries. Spread mixture into prepared pan, cover with clingfilm and freeze overnight.

Just before serving, toss remaining 125g raspberries with a little extra rose syrup. Slice semifreddo and serve with raspberries, scattered with mint sprigs. **Serves 6-8**

BAKED QUINCE WITH SWEET COUSCOUS

4 small quinces, peeled,
  quartered, cored
660g caster sugar
250ml dry white wine
2 cinnamon quills
1 star anise
12 small dried figs
100g couscous
2 tsp rosewater
1 tsp ground cinnamon
50g pistachios

If you've made the sweet couscous in advance, it might solidify due to the sugar syrup. To separate the grains, simply pulse a couple of times in a food processor.

Preheat the oven to 150°C (gas mark 2).

Place quince in a baking dish just large enough so they fit snugly. Reserve 1¹/₂ tbs sugar for couscous, then place remaining sugar in a saucepan over medium heat with wine, cinnamon, star anise and 500ml water, stirring until sugar dissolves. Pour sugar syrup over the quince, cover with foil and bake for 4 hours or until quince is tender and has turned a deep coral colour. Stir in the figs, then set aside to cool slightly.

Place couscous in a bowl. Combine rosewater, ground cinnamon and reserved 1¹/₂ tbs sugar in a saucepan with 125ml cold water. Bring to a simmer over medium-high heat, stirring until sugar dissolves. Pour over the couscous, cover with a clean tea towel, then set aside for 10 minutes. Fluff couscous with a fork and serve with baked quince and pistachios. **Serves 4**

PEACH TARTES FINES WITH PINK PEPPER ICE CREAM

1L good-quality vanilla
  ice cream
1 tbs pink peppercorns,
  crushed, plus extra
  to serve
110g caster sugar
2 bay leaves
1 vanilla bean, split
6 yellow peaches
1 quantity of quick puff
  pastry (see Essentials,
  p 165) or 2 sheets frozen
  puff pastry, thawed
Icing sugar, to dust

Adding crushed pink or black peppercorns to vanilla ice cream gives it an interesting, slightly floral, spicy flavour that really complements these peach tarts.

Soften ice cream slightly and stir through crushed peppercorns, then return to freezer until ready to serve.

Place caster sugar, bay leaves and vanilla in a saucepan with 1L water and bring to a simmer over medium-high heat, stirring until sugar dissolves. Add peaches, cover surface closely with a round of baking paper (cartouche), then reduce heat to medium-low and simmer for 5-10 minutes until tender (depending on the firmness of your peaches). Remove pan from heat and cool peaches in poaching liquid.

Preheat the oven to 180°C (gas mark 4). Line a heavy-based baking tray with baking paper.

If using homemade pastry, roll out to 5mm thick. Cut 6 x 12cm rounds from pastry and place on lined baking tray. Prick bases with a fork, then refrigerate until ready to assemble tarts.

Meanwhile, remove peaches from liquid and pat dry, then halve, remove stone and thinly slice. Fan out each sliced peach, slightly overlapping, over pastry rounds. Dust with icing sugar, then bake for 20 minutes or until the edges of the peaches are golden and pastry is crisp and cooked through.

Serve with pink peppercorn ice cream, scattered with extra peppercorns. **Serves 6**

dried CRANBERRIES

Mincemeat

Cinnamon quills

CHRISTMAS MORNING GRANOLA

180g rolled oats

75g unsalted mixed
   nuts of your choice,
   chopped if large

80g sunflower seeds

2 tbs sesame seeds

2 tbs shredded coconut

2 tbs extra virgin
   coconut oil

125ml cranberry juice

2 tbs dried cranberries

2 tbs chopped
   dried apricots

Milk, thick Greek-style
   yoghurt and 250g
   homemade mincemeat
   (see Essentials, p 284) or
   store-bought mincemeat,
   to serve

Preheat the oven to 150°C (gas mark 2).

Place oats, nuts, sunflower seeds, sesame seeds, shredded coconut, coconut oil and cranberry juice in a bowl and toss to combine. Spread onto a large baking tray and bake for 30 minutes, turning every 10 minutes, or until golden and dry. Cool, then toss with cranberries and apricots. Cool completely, then transfer to a sterilised jar. Store for up to 2 months.

Serve granola with milk, then top with a dollop each of yoghurt and mincemeat. **Serves 8-10**

BEETROOT GRAVLAX WITH HORSERADISH SNOW

600g raw beetroot
100g caster sugar
100g sea salt
80ml vodka
1 tbs soy sauce
800g-1kg centre-cut salmon
   fillet, skinned, pin-boned
100g creme fraiche
   or sour cream
1 tsp lemon juice
1 tsp fennel pollen
   (optional)
Extra virgin olive oil,
   to drizzle
30g piece fresh horseradish,
   peeled, frozen
Micro herbs and rye bread,
   to serve

Beetroot adds a beautiful scarlet tint to the salmon, and the horseradish 'snow' is a nod to this dish's Scandinavian origins. Begin this recipe 1 day ahead.

Set the smallest beetroot aside. Peel, then grate remaining beetroot and combine in a bowl with sugar, salt, vodka and soy sauce. Place half the mixture in a large, non-reactive glass or ceramic dish. Place salmon on top, then cover with remaining beetroot mixture. Cover with clingfilm and refrigerate for 12 hours.

Meanwhile, cook the reserved beetroot in a saucepan of boiling water until tender when pierced with a knife. Cool, then peel and cut into 1cm pieces. Cover and refrigerate until ready to serve.

Combine creme fraiche, lemon juice and pollen, if using, in a small bowl. Season with sea salt and freshly ground black pepper.

Wash the curing mixture off the salmon, then pat dry with paper towel. Thinly slice salmon and arrange on a platter. Drizzle over a little oil, then scatter over the diced beetroot and micro herbs. Just before serving, grate over the frozen horseradish. Serve with creme fraiche mixture and rye bread. **Serves 8-10**

PRAWN COCKTAIL CROSTINI

2 avocados

100ml buttermilk

Juice of 1 lemon

300g cooked peeled
  prawns (tails intact),
  deveined

150g mayonnaise (see
  Essentials, p 68) or
  store-bought whole-egg
  mayonnaise

2 tbs tomato ketchup

1 tsp Tabasco

12 slices chargrilled ciabatta

1 baby cos lettuce, outer
  leaves discarded

Cayenne pepper and dill,
  to serve

Using a blender, puree 1 avocado with the buttermilk and half
the lemon juice. Cut remaining avocado into 1cm pieces and
toss with the prawns and remaining lemon juice. Season with
sea salt and freshly ground black pepper.

Combine the mayonnaise, tomato ketchup and Tabasco in
a bowl and season.

Spread the ciabatta slices with a little of the avocado puree.
Top each with a lettuce leaf, then prawn mixture. Drizzle with
cocktail sauce, dust with cayenne and top with dill sprigs to serve.

Serves 6 as a starter

BRINED DUCK BREASTS
WITH STRAWBERRY SALSA

110g caster sugar
110g sea salt
4 x 200g duck breasts
   (skin on)
115g honey
2 tbs olive oil

Strawberry salsa
250g strawberries, hulled,
   finely chopped
2 shallots, finely chopped
2 tomatoes, seeds
   removed, finely chopped
2 tbs finely chopped
   mint leaves
2 tbs finely chopped
   coriander leaves
Finely grated zest and juice
   of 1 lime
1 jalapeno, seeds removed,
   finely chopped
1 tbs balsamic vinegar
2 tbs olive oil

Our friends in the USA have long known the benefits of brining. Soaking poultry in a salt and sugar solution overnight results in superbly moist and tender flesh. Begin this recipe 1 day ahead.

To make the brine, place sugar, salt and 1L of water in a large saucepan. Bring to the boil over medium-high heat, stirring until sugar and salt dissolve. Cool completely.

Place duck breasts in a plastic container, pour over the cooled brining liquid, then cover and refrigerate for 24 hours.

Preheat the oven to 170°C (gas mark 3).

Remove duck from brine and pat dry with paper towel, then place, skin-side down, in a cold frypan. Cook over medium heat for 5-6 minutes until the fat is rendered and the skin is golden. Transfer duck to the roasting pan, brush with honey and oil, then roast for 6 minutes for medium-rare or until cooked to your liking. Cover loosely with foil and rest for 6 minutes.

Meanwhile, to make salsa, combine all the ingredients in a bowl and season with sea salt and freshly ground black pepper.

Serve the duck breasts with strawberry salsa. **Serves 4**

ASIAN-GLAZED GAMMON

1.5-2kg gammon
    or part leg of ham
2 bay leaves
1 tbs chopped ginger
2 star anise
4 garlic cloves, bruised
Cucumber wedges,
    shredded long red chilli
    and coriander sprigs,
    to serve

Asian glaze
2 garlic cloves, bruised
Finely grated zest and juice
    of 1 orange
2 star anise
300g caster sugar
220g honey
60ml maple syrup
1 long red chilli,
    halved lengthways,
    seeds removed
100ml soy sauce

I was so excited to discover traditional gammon at my butcher's last Christmas. It's the meat from the hind legs of the pig, cured in a similar style to bacon. Unlike ham, it needs to be cooked before serving, but the flavour is so delicious, it's worth it, and it makes such a wonderful centrepiece for the Christmas table. This Asian glaze works just as well with a ham if you can't get gammon.

Place gammon in a large saucepan with bay leaves, ginger, star anise and garlic. Add enough cold water to cover, then bring to a simmer over medium-high heat, skimming the surface. Reduce heat to low, cover with a lid and simmer for 2½ hours.

Meanwhile, to make Asian glaze, place all the ingredients in a saucepan over low heat, stirring until sugar dissolves, then simmer, stirring occasionally, for 20-25 minutes until reduced and sticky.

Preheat the oven to 190°C (gas mark 5). Line a roasting pan with foil.

Remove gammon from poaching liquid and score the skin in a diamond pattern (this is purely decorative; alternatively, remove the skin and score the fat, which is edible). Place gammon on a wire rack set over the roasting pan. Brush generously with glaze, then roast for 35-40 minutes, basting every 10 minutes with glaze until the gammon is sticky and caramelised (check regularly towards the end of cooking as the glaze can burn easily).

Transfer to a platter and serve with cucumber wedges, shredded chilli and coriander sprigs. **Serves 6-8**

MINCEMEAT

Combine 250g raisins, 160g sultanas, 50g finely chopped dried apricots, 60g chopped glacé cherries, 75g mixed peel, 75g currants, 1 grated apple, 1 tsp each finely grated lemon and orange zest, 1 tbs lemon juice, 225g soft brown sugar, 1 tsp mixed spice, ¼ tsp grated nutmeg, 80ml brandy and 50g melted, cooled unsalted butter in a large bowl.

Transfer mixture to a food processor and pulse a few times until well combined.

Seal in an airtight container and store in a cool, dark place for up to 3 months.

For a longer shelf life, replace butter with 100g vegetable suet. Store in a screw-top jar for up to 1 year.

STUFFING

Heat 2 tbs olive oil in a frypan over medium heat.

Add 150g finely chopped bacon, 2 finely chopped onions and 3 finely chopped garlic cloves, then cook, stirring occasionally, until onion softens.

Transfer to a bowl, cool slightly, then add 2 tbs chopped sage leaves, 40g toasted pine nuts, finely grated zest of 1 lemon, 15g chopped flat-leaf parsley, 280g soft white breadcrumbs and 2 lightly beaten eggs.

Season well with sea salt and freshly ground pepper, then stir well with a wooden spoon.

Refrigerate to cool completely before stuffing the turkey.

SLOW-COOKED TURKEY WITH QUICK CRANBERRY SAUCE

4kg whole turkey
1 quantity of stuffing
  (see Essentials, p 285)
100g unsalted butter,
  melted
35g plain flour
80ml port
500ml chicken stock
Rosemary sprigs, to serve

Quick cranberry sauce
300ml port
120g caster sugar
125ml orange juice
400g frozen cranberries
2 tsp cornflour

Covering the turkey breast with a large piece of muslin soaked in butter will help prevent the meat from drying out, as well as giving the bird a beautifully crisp, golden skin.

Preheat the oven to 140°C (gas mark 1).

Rinse turkey in cold water, then pat dry inside and out with paper towel. Fill neck cavity with stuffing. Secure with toothpicks, then fill larger cavity with remaining stuffing. Truss legs with kitchen string.

Place turkey, breast-side up, on a wire rack set over a large roasting pan. Dip a large piece of muslin in melted butter and lay it over the turkey. Pour 2cm water into the roasting pan, then cover pan completely with foil. Roast for 4 hours, then remove foil, increase oven to 170°C (gas mark 3) and roast for a further 30-40 minutes until golden and juices run clear when the thickest part of the thigh is pierced. Remove from oven and rest, loosely covered with foil, for 20 minutes.

Meanwhile, to make gravy, place roasting pan over medium heat. Add flour and cook, stirring with a wooden spoon and scraping the cooked bits from the bottom of the pan, until golden. Add port and stir to combine. Add stock and bring to the boil, stirring, until mixture thickens slightly. Season with sea salt and freshly ground black pepper. Transfer to a jug. Keep warm.

While turkey is cooking, make cranberry sauce. Combine port, sugar and orange juice in a saucepan over medium heat, stirring until sugar dissolves. Add cranberries, reduce heat to low and cook for 8-10 minutes until fruit starts to burst. Combine cornflour with 2 tsp cold water in a small bowl, then add to cranberry mixture and stir until sauce thickens. Transfer to a serving bowl.

Serve turkey scattered with rosemary sprigs, with the cranberry sauce and gravy for guests to help themselves. **Serves 8-10**

PEA & HAM SALAD

3 smoked ham hocks

1 bay leaf

1 onion, roughly chopped

2 tbs extra virgin olive oil

1 tbs cider vinegar

2 tsp wholegrain mustard

160g fresh or 120g frozen
   peas, blanched, cooled

150g mangetout, trimmed,
   thinly sliced lengthways,
   blanched

150g sugar snap peas,
   trimmed, blanched

150g mangetout tendrils or
   picked watercress

150g flour, seasoned with
   sea salt and freshly
   ground black pepper

Olive oil, to shallow-fry

70g toasted flaked
   almonds

Ham hocks are readily available from supermarkets, so this recipe is for those who don't necessarily have leftovers from a Christmas ham. Here, the ham is matched with peas – one of my favourite combinations.

Place ham hocks, bay leaf and onion in a large saucepan. Add enough cold water to cover, then bring to the boil over medium-high heat, skimming the surface. Reduce heat to medium-low, cover with a lid and simmer for 2$\frac{1}{2}$ hours, topping up water if necessary. Remove ham hocks with tongs and set aside (discard poaching liquid and and solids). When cool enough to handle, remove ham meat in large chunks, discarding skin and bones.

Whisk together extra virgin olive oil, vinegar and mustard in a small bowl. Combine peas, mangetout, sugar snap peas, and mangetout tendrils on a platter.

Place seasoned flour in a shallow bowl. Heat 1cm olive oil in a frypan over high heat. Dust ham in flour, shaking off excess, then shallow-fry ham, in batches, until crisp and golden. Drain on paper towel.

To serve, drizzle salad with dressing, then scatter over ham and almonds. **Serves 6-8**

LAST-MINUTE CHRISTMAS PUDDINGS

600g mincemeat (see
   Essentials, p 284)
Finely grated zest
   of 1 orange
2 tbs brandy
50g plain flour
1 tsp mixed spice
50g soft white breadcrumbs
1 egg, lightly beaten
Single cream, to drizzle

Salted caramel
brandy butter
200g softened
   unsalted butter
250g dulce de leche
2 tbs brandy
1/2 tsp sea salt

You can make these lovely little puddings up to 2 weeks in advance; simply reheat them in their moulds for 30 minutes using the same method as below.

Grease 4 x 250ml dariole moulds and line the bases with a round of baking paper (this will help prevent sticking). Cut 4 rounds of baking paper and foil 3cm wider than the top of each mould.

Combine all ingredients, except cream, in a bowl and stir to combine. Divide mixture among moulds.

Make a small fold in the centre of each piece of baking paper and foil to allow for rising. Place a piece of pleated baking paper, then pleated foil, over each mould and secure with kitchen string. Place moulds in a saucepan just large enough to fit them snugly, then add enough boiling water to come halfway up the sides. Cover with a lid, bring to a simmer over medium-low heat, then reduce heat to low and simmer for 2¹/₂ hours, topping up with water if necessary, until cooked through.

To make salted caramel brandy butter, using a wooden spoon, beat together all the ingredients until well combined. Refrigerate until needed, then bring to room temperature before serving.

Serve puddings with salted caramel brandy butter, drizzled with a little cream. **Makes 4**

CHOCOLATE SILK TART WITH CHOCOLATE GLACÉ ORANGES

220g caster sugar
2 seedless oranges,
    thinly sliced
400g dark chocolate
    (70% cocoa solids),
    chopped, plus
    100g melted
1 quantity of store-bought
    chocolate pastry or sweet
    shortcrust pastry (see
    recipe, p 226)
400ml single cream
3 eggs, lightly beaten
60ml Grand Marnier or
    other orange liqueur

Chocolate glaze
80ml single cream
100g dark chocolate (70%
    cocoa solids), chopped
2 tsp liquid glucose
    or honey

Chocolate oranges have been a part of my family Christmas for as long as I can remember. Here, they make a perfect addition to a rich chocolate tart.

Preheat oven to 120°C (gas mark 1/2). Line a large baking tray with baking paper.

To make chocolate glacé oranges, place sugar and 250ml water in a saucepan. Stir over low heat until sugar dissolves, then increase heat to medium and simmer for a further 2-3 minutes until slightly reduced. Remove from heat, add orange slices and set aside to cool completely. Transfer to the lined baking tray and place in oven for 4 hours until crisp and dry. Half-dip each slice in melted chocolate and cool on a wire rack.

Meanwhile, increase the oven to 190°C (gas mark 5). Grease a 20cm x 30cm loose-bottomed tart pan.

Roll out pastry to 5mm thick and use to line tart pan. Refrigerate for 30 minutes. Prick tart base with a fork, then line with baking paper and fill with rice or pastry weights. Bake for 10 minutes, then remove paper and weights, and cook for a further 2 minutes or until crisp and dry. Reduce the oven to 170°C (gas mark 3).

Place cream in a saucepan over medium heat and bring to just below boiling point. Place chocolate in a bowl and pour over cream. Stand until chocolate melts, then stir until smooth. Add eggs and liqueur, then stir to combine. Pour into tart shell, then bake for 20 minutes or until just set. Cool in pan.

To make glaze, heat cream in a small saucepan over low heat for 1-2 minutes until hot. Place the chocolate and glucose in a bowl, then pour over cream. Stand until chocolate melts, then stir until smooth. Cool slightly, then pour over tart, tilting tart to spread glaze evenly. Refrigerate for 15 minutes to set glaze.

Serve the chocolate tart with chocolate glacé oranges. **Serves 8**

ICED YOGHURT PARFAIT WITH SPICED CHERRY SAUCE

220g caster sugar
2 egg whites
250g thick Greek yoghurt
1 tbs lemon juice
125ml double cream,
   whisked to
   soft peaks with
   1 tsp vanilla extract
Amaretti biscuits, to serve

Spiced cherry sauce
55g caster sugar
80ml cranberry juice or
   water
1 cinnamon quill
2 star anise
375g fresh pitted or frozen
   cherries
1½ tsp arrowroot

Begin this recipe 1 day ahead.

Line a 2L terrine or square cake pan with clingfilm.

Place caster sugar and 250ml water in a saucepan over low heat, stirring until the sugar dissolves. Increase the heat to medium and simmer for a further 5 minutes or until slightly reduced.

Meanwhile, whisk the egg whites in the clean bowl of an electric mixer to soft peaks. Whisking constantly, slowly pour in the hot syrup. Continue whisking until mixture has cooled.

Combine the yoghurt and lemon juice in a large bowl. Fold in the whipped cream mixture, then gently fold in meringue mixture. Spoon mixture into the prepared terrine and freeze overnight.

To make the spiced cherry sauce, place the sugar and cranberry juice in a small saucepan over a low heat, stirring until sugar dissolves. Add cinnamon, star anise and cherries, then cook for 5-6 minutes until the cherries release their juices.

Combine the arrowroot with 2 tbs cold water and add to the sauce. Cook for a further 1 minute or until slightly thickened. Cool, then refrigerate until ready to use.

To serve, use the clingfilm to lift the parfait out of the terrine or cake pan onto a board. Slice, drizzle with the spiced cherry sauce and crumble over the amaretti biscuits. **Serves 6**

MENUS

ARABIAN NIGHT

SUNDAY ROAST WITH A TWIST

ASIAN SUMMER LUNCH

MEXICAN FIESTA

LIGHT AND BREEZY

MIDWEEK ENTERTAINING

FAMILY GATHERING

ALFRESCO LUNCH

INDEX

MEAT

PASTA, RICE & NOODLES

VEGETABLES

SALADS

DESSERTS

CAKES & BAKES

FRUIT

FESTIVE

ESSENTIALS

EXTRAS

THANKS

This book, like the others that have come before it, is only possible because of the amazing group of people I work alongside.

My thanks go to the management team at NewsLifeMedia, especially Nicole Sheffield and Fiona Nilsson, as well as the team at ABC Books and HarperCollins, particularly Shona Martyn and Brigitta Doyle, who always offer nothing but positive encouragement.

The beautiful images are the work of photographer Jeremy Simons, who has captured the essence of *delicious.* so perfectly. Food stylist David Morgan, in my opinion, is the best in the business and takes my recipes to another level with his eye for detail. You always go the extra mile, David, and for that I am truly grateful.

The entire book has been a collaborative effort by the fantastic people I work with on the magazine. Warren Mendes joined our food team as assistant food editor just before we started work on this book (talk about a baptism of fire!) and his great food knowledge and organisational skills have made such a difference. I'm indebted to him for all his hard work, both for his cooking on the shoots and his recipe editing. Food assistant Sarah Murphy, whose title doesn't do justice to all the work she does, has been tireless in ensuring we had the best produce to work with, and that each day's shoot ran smoothly.

I've always called editor Danielle Oppermann my rock, and your guidance and support, as always, have been invaluable. Project editor Sally Feldman has worked diligently to ensure that every word is perfect, and I can't thank you enough for all your input. We were so lucky to have Anita Jokovich as project art director. I love everything you've done to make this book so beautiful, and thanks especially for the hours you spent handwriting all those recipe titles (I owe you a few hand massages!). The lovely illustrations that make this book so unique are the work of Elizabeth Lough, *delicious.* magazine's senior designer.

Thanks also to chief subeditor Shannon Harley for reading every page and adding her wisdom, and to art director Shannon Keogh, who has been so integral to the creative process from start to finish. In fact, everyone on the magazine team has played a part, so thanks also to Yasmin Newman, Heidi Finnane and Amy Pagett.

And last but not least, to my family, Phil, Toby and Henry. You know how I *Love to Cook* for you, so I'm dedicating this one to you.

This edition first published in the UK in 2014 by Quadrille Publishing Ltd.
www.quadrille.co.uk

First published in Australia in 2013 by HarperCollins*Publishers* Australia Pty Limited, ABN 36 009 913 517 harpercollins.com.au

HarperCollins*Publishers*
Level 13, 201 Elizabeth St, Sydney NSW 2000, Australia; 31 View Rd, Glenfield, Auckland 0627, NZ; A 53, Sector 57, Noida, UP, India; 77–85 Fulham Palace Rd, London W6 8JB, UK; 2 Bloor Street East, 20th floor, Toronto, Ontario M4W 1A8, Canada; 10 East 53rd St, New York NY 10022, USA

Food Director Valli Little   **Photography** Jeremy Simons (Andy Lewis pp 248-249, 267)   **Styling** David Morgan
Art Director Shannon Keogh
Project Art Director Anita Jokovich
Editor Danielle Oppermann   **Project Editor** Sally Feldman
Chief Subeditor Shannon Harley   **Illustrations** Elizabeth Lough
Food preparation Warren Mendes and Sarah Murphy

Colour reproduction by Graphic Print Group, Adelaide, SA

ISBN 978 184949 529 5

Printed and bound in China